Outdoor Furniture
FOR THE Backyard Builder

AMERICAN WOODWORKER.

OUTDOOR FURNITURE
FOR THE Backyard Builder

Easy-to-Build Projects for the Yard and Deck

BILL HYLTON with *Fred Matlack and Phil Gehret*
Illustrations by Frank Rohrbach
Photos by Mitch Mandel

Reader's® Digest

THE READER'S DIGEST ASSOCIATION, INC.
Pleasantville, New York/Montreal

The author and editors who compiled this book have tried to make all of the contents as accurate and as correct as possible. Plans, illustrations, photographs, and text have all been carefully checked and cross-checked. However, due to the variability of local conditions, construction materials, personal skill, and so on, neither the author nor Reader's Digest assumes any responsibility for any injuries suffered or for damages or other losses incurred that result from the material presented herein. All instructions and plans should be carefully studied and clearly understood before beginning construction.

American Woodworker is a registered trademark of RD Publications, Inc.

Printed in the United States of America.

Library of Congress Cataloging in Publication Data
Hylton, Bill.
    [Outdoor Furniture.   Selections]
    Outdoor furniture for the backyard builder : easy-to-build projects for the yard and deck /
Bill Hylton with Fred Matlack and Phil Gehret ; illustrations by Frank Rohrbach ; photos by
Mitch Mandel.
       p.   cm.
    ISBN 0-7621-0180-6
    1. Outdoor furniture--Design and construction.   2. Garden ornaments and furniture--Design
and construction.   3. Furniture making. I. Matlack, Fred. II. Gehret, Phil. III. Title.
TT197.5.09H962 1999
684.1'8—dc21   99-24916

On the front cover: A view of the Adirondack Settee, found on page 88. *On the back cover:* The Chair, Bench, and Swing from the Contoured Ensemble, found on page 54, and the Picnic Table and Benches in the Round, found on page 42.

If you have any questions or comments concerning the editorial content of this book, please write to:

Reader's Digest
Illustrated Reference Books Editors
Reader's Digest Road
Pleasantville, NY 10570

You can also visit us on the World Wide Web at http://www.readersdigest.com

4 6 8 10 9 7 5

CONTENTS

INTRODUCTION

When you think of outdoor furniture, what comes to mind? A picnic table, right? Maybe an Adirondack chair, or a redwood lounger. If you want that type of furniture, this is the book for you. It's a collection of easy-to-build traditional outdoor furniture.

Prove it to yourself. Go ahead: Flip through the pages, if you haven't already. Check out what the book has to show you. You'll see several different picnic tables. You'll see a classic Adirondack chair and ottoman. You'll see an ensemble of redwood furniture, including a chair and settee, a lounger, and a folding table. And you'll see some surprise projects that go beyond the expected.

Whether you are an experienced woodworker or a home handyman willing to tackle some real woodworking, this is your ticket to affordable outdoor furniture. Many of the projects can be built with a circular saw and a drill/driver. Work right on the deck or patio, where you'll eventually use the furniture. And if you've got a table saw or a radial arm saw, if you've got a router, you can build the more challenging projects, like the impressive, solid-oak Acadia bench and chair.

In creating this book, our two goals were to provide an interesting, exciting mix of furniture projects—something for every taste, budget, and skill level—and to present each project in thorough, lucid detail. Assuming that you already have a book or two on woodworking, we included nothing in *OUTDOOR FURNITURE FOR THE BACKYARD BUILDER* but projects. There's no chapter on techniques, no appendix with a rundown on tools or joints or glues.

It's just projects.

And what a showcase of outdoor furniture. When we designed this small collection, we wanted classy, comfortable, practical, *durable* outdoor stuff.

You want a picnic table? We've got an all-in-one unit, a round table with stools, a rectangular table with a diagonal-stripped top. There's even one you can fold up for storage.

Feel a need to relax? Settle back in our traditional porch rocker. Or gently rock yourself and a companion in the glider. Or swing in the oak porch swing.

How about lounging in the sun? There's a fixed-back oak chaise lounge and a redwood 2 × 4 version with a reclining back.

For every piece of furniture, there's a style to suit every taste, and there's a variety of constructions to accommodate—or challenge—any skill level and tool inventory. The California Redwood Ensemble (of chair, settee, chaise lounge, and folding table) requires only a drill/driver and a circular saw to complete, but the Acadia bench and chair can't be built outside of a well-equipped shop.

The project presentations are shaped to serve a diversity of needs. Skim through the pages again: Highlighted tips and how-to photos present timesaving shortcuts and proven techniques you can use in *any project*. Page more slowly: Photos show what the finished projects look like in typical backyard settings. "Builder's Notes" discuss the salient aspects of every project. Where a specific tool or glue or finish is pertinent to the project, detailed information about it is presented in the notes. Tool and shopping lists let you know what tools are necessary and how much wood is required; you won't get started on a project that you can't complete.

Once you do start, the information you need is all there. Dimensioned drawings, gridded patterns, isolated details—we've got scores of revealing and helpful two-color drawings. Clarifying important woodworking operations and assembly procedures are dozens of how-to photos. Step-by-step directions list the work sequence and describe *how* to do the tasks necessary to build each project. All of these features support you novices or weekend woodworkers as you build a project.

As for those of you who are veteran woodworkers, who don't need—or want—all the guidance, you can simply peruse the Cutting List and dimensioned illustrations and set to work. If a technique is unfamiliar, the explanation is there.

And don't assume that there are no challenges in *OUTDOOR FURNITURE FOR THE BACKYARD BUILDER*. The Acadia bench and chair is handsome and expensive-looking, with its mortise-and-tenon construction in solid oak.

Bill Hylton has been writing and editing Rodale Press books for more than 20 years. He created Rodale's first woodworking title, *Build It Better Yourself*, as well as its most recent backyard building title, *Projects for Outdoor Living*. **Fred Matlack** and **Phil Gehret** have been building projects for Rodale's magazines and books for 15 years. They've designed and constructed hundreds of projects, ranging from solar food driers to toys to antique reproductions. All the projects in *OUTDOOR FURNITURE FOR THE BACKYARD BUILDER* were designed and constructed by Fred 'n' Phil.

CALIFORNIA REDWOOD ENSEMBLE

A Super Set from a Weekend's Work

Easy as this set is to build, it offers a lot of action: The lounger's a mobile recliner, the table folds for storage, and even the chair and settee can be hung in a glider stand for some easy swingin'.

CALIFORNIA REDWOOD ENSEMBLE CHAIR AND SETTEE

The motivating concept behind these outdoor seats, and behind the lounger and table that complement them, is "Quick and Easy." What could be more contemporary!

Eschewing their stationary power tools, Rodale woodworkers Fred Matlack and Phil Gehret created a collection of pieces that are made with a standard lumberyard stock, using home-handyman power tools. The pieces are easy to build in almost no time at all. Perfect backyard projects for the weekend woodworker.

The chair is the foundation of the ensemble, and it displays the aesthetic and engineering motifs characteristic of the whole ensemble: redwood 2 × 4 lumber, simply tapered legs supporting a slatted seat and backrest, and basic butt-joint construction fastened with the increasingly popular galvanized drywall-type screw.

The settee is simply a wider version of the chair—the back slats, seat slats, and apron are longer on the settee than on the chair, but the side assemblies are identical. The building procedures are the same for both pieces. And either can be accommodated in the optional glider stand.

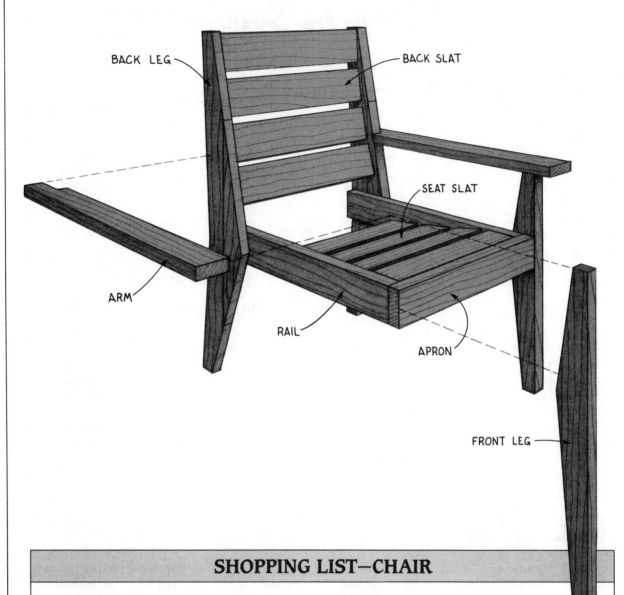

SHOPPING LIST—CHAIR

LUMBER

5 pcs. 2 × 4 × 8' construction heart redwood

HARDWARE AND SUPPLIES

42 pcs. #6 × 3" galvanized drywall-type screws
10 pcs. #6 × 2" galvanized drywall-type screws

FINISH

Clear water repellent or clear exterior finish

SHOPPING LIST—SETTEE

LUMBER

8 pcs. 2 × 4 × 8' construction heart redwood

HARDWARE AND SUPPLIES

42 pcs. #6 × 3" galvanized drywall-type screws
10 pcs. #6 × 2" galvanized drywall-type screws

FINISH

Clear water repellent or clear exterior finish

CUTTING LIST—CHAIR

PIECE	NUMBER	THICKNESS	WIDTH	LENGTH	MATERIAL
Back legs*	2	1½"	3½"	36"	Redwood
Back leg tapers*	2	1½"	3½"	24"	Redwood
Front legs	2	1½"	3½"	22½"	Redwood
Rails	2	1½"	3½"	23"	Redwood
Seat slats	4	1½"	3½"	19"	Redwood
Apron	1	1½"	3½"	22"	Redwood
Back slats	4	1½"	3½"	22"	Redwood
Arms	2	1½"	3½"	27"	Redwood

*Cut the back legs and back leg tapers from 2 × 8 stock to avoid edge-joining 2 × 4s.

CUTTING LIST—SETTEE

PIECE	NUMBER	THICKNESS	WIDTH	LENGTH	MATERIAL
Back legs*	2	1½"	3½"	36"	Redwood
Back leg tapers*	2	1½"	3½"	24"	Redwood
Front legs	2	1½"	3½"	22½"	Redwood
Rails	2	1½"	3½"	23"	Redwood
Seat slats	4	1½"	3½"	41"	Redwood
Apron	1	1½"	3½"	44"	Redwood
Back slats	4	1½"	3½"	44"	Redwood
Arms	2	1½"	3½"	27"	Redwood

*Cut the back legs and back leg tapers from 2 × 8 stock to avoid edge-joining 2 × 4s.

Builder's Notes

Three characteristics dominate this project from the builder's perspective. First, it is made of redwood, long the traditional wood for outdoor projects. Second, it is joined in simple butt joints secured with screws. (No, glue isn't necessary.) Third, it is a hand and portable power tool project.

Materials. Redwood is the traditional choice for outdoor projects because of its natural beauty and weatherability. In fact, commercial outdoor furniture made of other woods is often stained to give it a "redwood look." This rugged ensemble is made from the real thing, and it would be the ideal group to furnish a redwood deck.

Though redwood is naturally resistant to weather's punishment, only the darker-colored heartwood (cut from the center portion of the tree) resists decay; the lighter, cream-colored sapwood does not. When selecting lumber, avoid pieces that contain sapwood.

For this project, we used construction heart redwood. This grade contains a few knots and other slight defects but is much less expensive than clear all-heart redwood.

Unless you live on the West Coast, your local lumberyard may not stock redwood in sizes other than standard 2 × 4s. The ensemble was designed with this limitation in mind—note that we edge-joined two pieces of 2 × 4 stock to achieve the required 7-inch width for the back legs of the chair and settee. To avoid making this splice, cut the back legs from 2 × 8 stock if it's available in your area.

(There *are* alternatives, of course. You can use cedar, which is a good "outdoor" lumber, though it is soft and easily dented. And think seriously about plain old Douglas fir. It is considerably less expensive than redwood. Given a sound outdoor finish—one that you maintain year after year—the entire ensemble will last for decades.)

The screws used to fasten the parts of the chair and

CUTTING DIAGRAM—CHAIR

2 x 4 x 8'

BACK LEG	BACK LEG	FRONT LEG

2 x 4 x 8'

BACK LEG TAPER	BACK LEG TAPER	FRONT LEG	RAIL

2 x 4 x 8'

RAIL	APRON	BACK SLAT	BACK SLAT

2 x 4 x 8'

ARM	ARM	BACK SLAT	SEAT SLAT

2 x 4 x 8'

BACK SLAT	SEAT SLAT	SEAT SLAT	SEAT SLAT	

CUTTING DIAGRAM—SETTEE

2 x 4 x 8'

BACK LEG	BACK LEG	FRONT LEG

2 x 4 x 8'

BACK LEG TAPER	BACK LEG TAPER	FRONT LEG	RAIL

2 x 4 x 8'

RAIL	ARM	ARM	

2 x 4 x 8'

APRON	SEAT SLAT	

2 x 4 x 8'

SEAT SLAT	SEAT SLAT	

2 x 4 x 8'

SEAT SLAT	BACK SLAT	

2 x 4 x 8'

BACK SLAT	BACK SLAT	

2 x 4 x 8'

BACK SLAT	

settee are the drywall type. Designed to be driven with a power screwdriver, they have a profile and thread pitch calculated to expedite power driving. Its bugle-shaped head is billed as being self-countersinking, and to a large extent it is. The particular screws we used are galvanized; they are often packaged as "decking screws" or "all-purpose screws." Although they are more expensive than nails, they hold better than nails.

Be sure you purchase galvanized screws intended for exterior use. And always drill pilot holes for the screws, so the wood doesn't split.

Tools and techniques. This is very much a circular-saw project. The primary guideline was to design an ensemble that could be constructed using typical hand and portable power tools. No table saws, no band saws, no drill presses. Just something to build on a spring weekend.

A nearly essential tool is a drill-driver. You'll need forearms like Popeye if you expect to drive all the screws in the chair and settee by hand. Best bet: a drill fitted with a pilot hole bit in one hand, a drill-driver with a Phillips bit in the other. Where the directions call for a very deep countersink, remember that redwood is relatively soft and that, with the torque of a drill-driver forcing it, the screw itself can create a countersink. In other words, countersink the pilot hole as deep as you can, then drive the screw as deep as you can.

Finish. When your chair and settee are completed, they'll look great. But a finish can prolong their attractiveness and their structural integrity by mollifying the effects of sunlight and moisture on the wood.

Curiously, the finish we ultimately applied enhances the strength of redwood—its resistance to the effects of moisture—but does relatively little to bolster its resistance to the effects of sunlight. The heart of redwood is naturally rot-resistant. Moreover, because it is a very light (not dense) wood, it is relatively resistant to cupping and splitting. But sunlight will turn the wood gray.

The challenge here is to find a finish that protects your redwood furniture without concealing its inherent beauty. Presuming you want to keep it looking natural, you can eliminate paint and stains from consideration,

TOOL LIST

Backsaw	Ruler
Bar clamps	Saber saw
Circular saw	Sander(s)
Drill	Sandpaper
Pilot hole bit	Sawhorses
Framing square	Screwdriver
Level	Tack cloth
Paintbrush	Tape measure
Router	Try square
¼" rounding-over bit	Yardstick

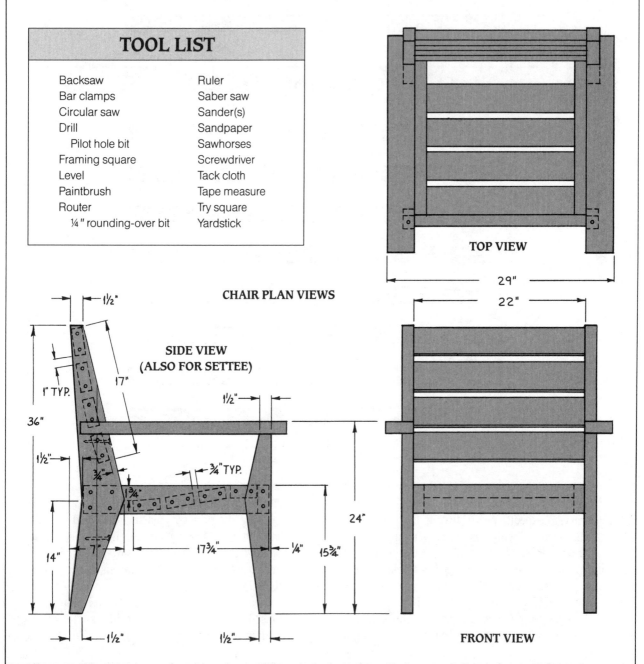

CHAIR PLAN VIEWS

TOP VIEW

29"

22"

**SIDE VIEW
(ALSO FOR SETTEE)**

1½"

1" TYP.

17"

36"

1½"

¾"

¾"

1¾"

¾" TYP.

1¾"

14"

7"

17¾"

¼"

15¾"

24"

1½"

1½"

1½"

FRONT VIEW

even though these are the finishes that protect most effectively against photodegradation (the degrading effects of the sun).

So what did we use? A plain water repellent.

Water repellents are popular for applications where you want to retain the natural appearance of wood while protecting it from cracking and warping. They contain no pigment and darken the wood only slightly. The first application to smooth surfaces is usually short-lived. When a blotchy discoloration starts to show, the wood should be cleaned with a liquid household bleach and detergent solution, then re-treated. During the first few years, retreatment will be an annual affair. But after the wood has weathered to a uniform color, it will need refinishing only when it becomes discolored by fungi.

To prevent mildew and fungi that can discolor the surface, use a water-repellent preservative, which is a water repellent that contains a fungicide. Because this is only a surface treatment, the fungicide will not prevent rot.

Alternative finishes include exterior-grade penetrating oils and exterior-grade varnishes.

SETTEE PLAN VIEWS

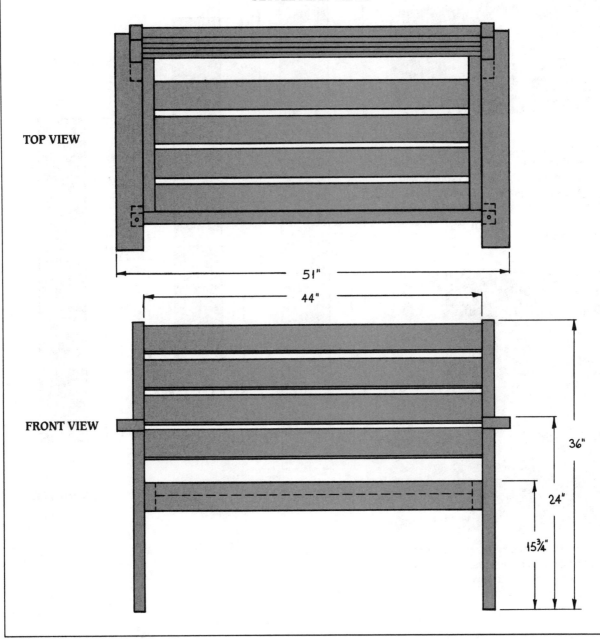

TOP VIEW

51"

FRONT VIEW

44"

36"

24"

15¾"

1. **Make the back and front legs.** Cut stock to length for the front and back legs, then lay out and cut the tapers on each, as shown in the *Leg Layout*.

The back legs are assembled by edge-joining the two pieces with 3-inch-long screws. Drill pilot holes for the fasteners, countersinking them deeply, as shown in the *Side View*. Using a router and a ¼-inch rounding-over bit, radius all legs.

Outside tapers for the front and back legs can be cut with a circular saw. To do this safely, clamp the workpiece to a long 2 × 4 supported on sawhorses. Set your saw to *just* break through the workpiece, so you don't unduly weaken the support board. You'll have to reposition the clamp after the initial cut.

Support the pieces for the back legs on sawhorses, and cut the inside tapers with a saber saw. Equip the saw with the widest blade you have to ensure the cut is straight and true.

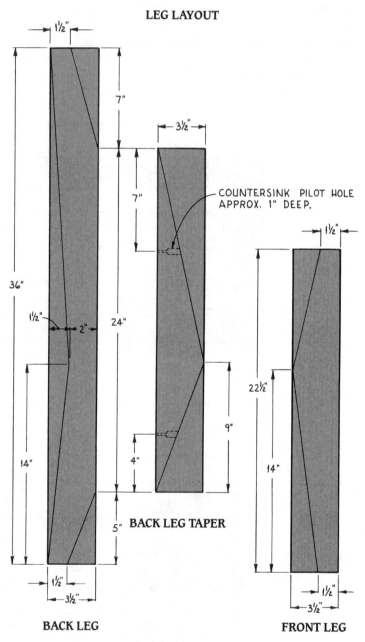

LEG LAYOUT

COUNTERSINK PILOT HOLE APPROX. 1" DEEP.

BACK LEG

BACK LEG TAPER

FRONT LEG

2. Make the seat.

2. Make the seat. Cut the rails, seat slats, and apron to length. Radius all exposed edges.

The seat slats form a slight curve, as shown in the *Side View*. Using the drawing as a guide, mark the positions of the front and rear seat slats on the inside faces of the rails. Flex a thin strip of scrap—¼-inch plywood, plastic laminate, even a thin yardstick—to form a curve connecting the positions of the front and rear slats, and scribe the curve on the rail. (An extra pair of hands makes this as easy to do as it is to say.) When both rails are marked, lay out the positions of the middle two seat slats, spacing them approximately ¾ inch apart.

Drill pilot holes, then drive 3-inch screws through the rails into the ends of the seat slats. Fasten the apron to the front ends of the rails in the same manner.

3. Fasten the legs to the seat assembly.

3. Fasten the legs to the seat assembly. Start by marking the rail location on the inside of the legs; refer to the *Side View* for this information. Lay a front leg and a back leg on the benchtop. Stand the seat assembly on edge, positioning the rail on top of the legs.

Fasten the back leg first. Drill a pilot hole, then drive a single 2-inch screw through the rail and into the leg. Then use a framing square and long straightedge to square up the leg to the rail, and drive three more screws into the joint. The front leg is "tacked" in place with a single screw.

Repeat the process to install the second back leg and to tack the second front leg in place. Set the chair (or settee) on its feet now, square up the front legs with a framing square, and drive additional screws through the legs into the rails.

Above: A framing square and straightedge, used as shown, help you "square up" the back legs to the seat. A single screw holds the parts in position, yet enables you to pivot the leg to square it up.

Right: To square up the front legs, hang the framing square from the rail. This enables you to square up the front leg with one hand and drive screws with the other.

4. **Fasten the back slats to the back legs.** You need to position the slats on the legs so the backrest is slightly curved. On the inside of the back legs, mark the locations of the top and bottom back slats, as shown in the *Side View*. As with the seat, use a flexible strip to establish the arc between the top and bottom slats, and scribe it on the legs.

Install the top slat first. Drill pilot holes and drive two 3-inch screws through the legs into each end of the slat. Repeat the process to install the other three slats.

TIP

Use a tourniquet-type clamp—sometimes called a Spanish windlass—to hold the back slats in position while you drill pilot holes and drive screws. The tourniquet pulls the legs together, pinching the slat and holding it in place. To make the tourniquet, simply loop a piece of sturdy twine around the legs, then use a short stick to twist the twine, as shown. This arrangement has two advantages: It's far cheaper than a long bar clamp or pipe clamp, and it won't leave jaw marks on the wood.

5. **Fasten the arms to the legs.** Cut the arms to length, and radius all the exposed edges. The arms must be scribed and notched to fit around the back legs, as shown in the *Top View*. To scribe an arm for cutting, rest it on the front leg, butt it against the side of the leg, and mark the angle of the back leg on it. Make sure the arm is level from front to back. Cut the notch with a backsaw or hand saw.

Fasten each arm to the legs by driving 3-inch screws through the arm into the front leg and 2-inch screws through the back leg into the arm.

To mark the notch where the arm fits around the back leg, rest the arm on the front leg, line it up against the back leg, and run a pencil along the edge of the leg, marking the arm. You can level the arm visually, as done here, or with more exactitude by resting a level on the arm.

6. **Apply a finish.** Sand the entire piece with fine-grit sandpaper, smoothing any sharp or splintery edges. Apply the clear finish of your choice and let it dry. Now, sit down and relax—it's done!

CALIFORNIA REDWOOD GLIDER STAND

What is it about gliders that evokes nostalgic feelings? It's a wistful image. The spacious porch with gaudy striped awnings. A cooling breeze coming just at dusk. Murmuring voices, comforting voices. The creak of the glider.

Is it the gentle rocking? Is it the creaking of the wood and the pivots? Even people who never had a porch feel it.

Well, whatever it is, with this glider stand, you can have it, too. Embue your California redwood settee with that nostalgic—and very pleasant—quality. If you've successfully completed the settee, you'll find the stand easy to build.

The glider stand doesn't have to be restricted to the settee, of course. By shortening the cross members, you can make it accommodate the chair.

SHOPPING LIST

LUMBER

2 pcs. 2 × 4 × 8' construction heart redwood
1 pc. 2 × 4 × 10' construction heart redwood

HARDWARE AND SUPPLIES

28 pcs. #6 × 3" galvanized drywall-type screws
1 pc. ⅛" × ¾" × 72" steel strap
1 pc. ½" × ½" × 60" aluminum channel

HARDWARE AND SUPPLIES—CONTINUED

8 pcs. ¼" × 2" hex-head bolts, washers, and locknuts
8 pcs. #6 × ½" roundhead wood screws

FINISH

Clear water repellent or clear exterior finish

CUTTING LIST

PIECE	NUMBER	THICKNESS	WIDTH	LENGTH	MATERIAL
Legs	4	1½"	3½"	23"	Redwood
Bottom rails	2	1½"	3½"	25"	Redwood
Top rails	2	1½"	3½"	27"	Redwood
Cross members	2	1½"	3½"	49"	Redwood

CUTTING DIAGRAM

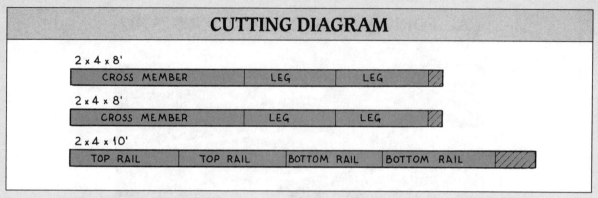

2 x 4 x 8'

| CROSS MEMBER | LEG | LEG | |

2 x 4 x 8'

| CROSS MEMBER | LEG | LEG | |

2 x 4 x 10'

| TOP RAIL | TOP RAIL | BOTTOM RAIL | BOTTOM RAIL | |

GLIDER STAND PLAN VIEWS

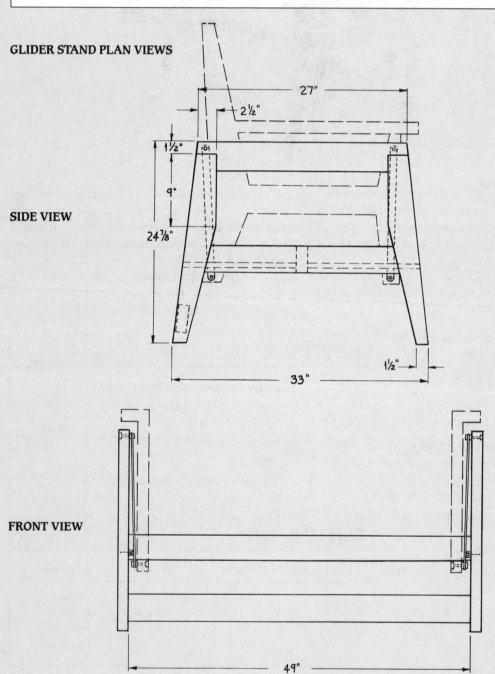

SIDE VIEW

27"

2½"

1½"

9"

24⅞"

1½"

33"

FRONT VIEW

49"

Builder's Notes

The glider stand consists of two identical side frames, joined by two cross members. You hang the settee in the stand by means of four metal supports, which allow the swinging action. Use the same materials for the stand that you used for the chair and settee. The tool requirements and the techniques you use are essentially the same, too.

To complete the glider, build the settee on page 4, but cut 4 inches off the bottom of each leg. This maintains the settee's height, yet allows attachment to the stand, as shown in the *Side View*. Most important, it provides the ground clearance necessary for swinging.

<table>
<tr><td colspan="2" align="center">TOOL LIST</td></tr>
<tr><td>Bar clamps</td><td>Router</td></tr>
<tr><td>Centerpunch</td><td>¼" rounding-over bit</td></tr>
<tr><td>Circular saw</td><td>Ruler</td></tr>
<tr><td>Drill</td><td>Saber saw</td></tr>
<tr><td>¼" dia. bit (for metal)</td><td>Sander(s)</td></tr>
<tr><td>¾" dia. spade bit</td><td>Sandpaper</td></tr>
<tr><td>Countersink bit</td><td>Sawhorses</td></tr>
<tr><td>Pilot hole bit</td><td>Screwdriver</td></tr>
<tr><td>File</td><td>Tack cloth</td></tr>
<tr><td>Hacksaw</td><td>Tape measure</td></tr>
<tr><td>Hammer</td><td>Try square</td></tr>
<tr><td>Paintbrush</td><td>Wrench</td></tr>
</table>

1. Cut and assemble the legs and rails. Lay out and cut the four legs, as shown in the *Leg Layout*. You can lay out each leg individually, or just lay out one and, after cutting the tapers and mitering the ends, use it as a template to lay out the others. In any case, cut the tapers with a circular saw; clamp the leg to a 2 × 4 supported on sawhorses to safely manage this operation.

Cut the lower rails to size, mitering the ends at a 75 degree angle, as shown in the *Side View*. Lay out the top rails, as shown in the *Top Rail Layout,* and cut them out. Use a saber saw to cut the notches.

The legs and rails are fastened together with deeply countersunk 3-inch screws. To ensure that the completed assemblies are flat and true (as opposed to wracked or twisted), set them in position on a workbench, then clamp them to the benchtop (but not to each other). With the pieces clamped down, drill pilot holes through the edges of the legs into the ends of the rails (see the *Side View*), countersinking the holes as much as 1¾ inches. Drive the screws.

Complete the work on these assemblies by radiusing all exposed edges.

LEG AND TOP RAIL LAYOUTS

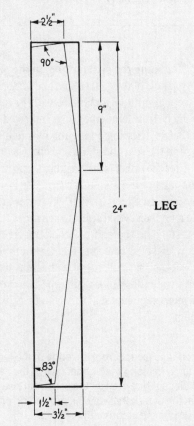

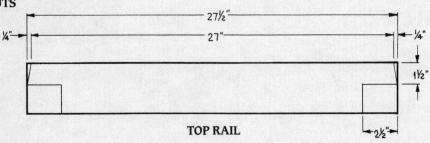

2. **Join the two leg-and-rail assemblies.** Cut the cross members and radius all four sides. To join the two leg-and-rail assemblies, position the cross members, as shown in the *Side View* and *Front View*. After drilling pilot holes, drive 3-inch screws through the back legs and the bottom rails into the ends of the cross members.

3. **Make the metal supports and rub rails.** From the ⅛-inch by ¾-inch steel strap, cut four 17-inch pieces. Radius the ends with a file or grinder, and drill ¼-inch-diameter holes at each end, as indicated in the *Side View*. From the ½-inch by ½-inch aluminum channel, cut four rub rails 14½ inches long. There are two rub rails attached to each bottom rail, one on each side of the center cross member. Spray paint both sides of these metal pieces (rub rails *and* supports) with a rust-preventive paint before assembly.

> ### TIP
>
> Mark the center of each hole you drill in metal with a centerpunch and hammer. The centerpunch will dimple the metal, and this tiny depression will prevent the drill bit from wandering across the metal surface as you start the drill.

4. **Hang the seat (settee) in the glider stand.** In the top rails of the glider stand and bottom ends of the seat (settee), drill ¼-inch holes with ¾-inch-diameter by ¼-inch-deep counterbores, as indicated in the *Front View*. Before screwing on the rub rails and hanging the seat, sand the seat and stand and apply a finish to both.

After the finish is dry, install the rub rails along the bottom rails of the stand (see the *Side View*). Use four equally spaced screws in each. Drill holes in the rub rails for the roundhead wood screws, then screw them in place.

Fasten the top end of each support to the glider stand with bolts, washers, and locknuts. Then, using scrap blocks of wood to raise the seat to the correct height inside the stand, fasten the bottom ends of the metal supports to the seat legs with bolts, washers, and locknuts.

The rub rails extend from the edge of the legs (front and back) in along the bottom rails to the center crosspiece. They prevent the seat from swaying side to side in the stand; that way the protruding pivot bolts can't gouge the stand or the seat.

CALIFORNIA REDWOOD ENSEMBLE CHAISE LOUNGE

This reclining chaise is a natural complement to the California Redwood Ensemble, but it doesn't always have to stick to the group. Unlike the chairs and table, it has wheels, so it can easily be moved to the sunny spot. With its reclining back, it was designed for sunbathing.

The special hardware that supports the backrest is nifty. Because of its similarity to the principle of the cog railway, we're calling the hardware pieces cog-latch braces. Just as the railway's cog system prevents the train from slipping back as it advances up a steep grade, so do these braces prevent the backrest from dropping back. As you raise the backrest, a latch engages a cog, maintaining the backrest's position. To drop it into the fully reclining position, you must raise it up as far as it will go, *then* lower it.

Just as it is easy to build, the lounger is easy to use. Roll it to the sunny spot, lift the back a click or two, stretch out, and just broil.

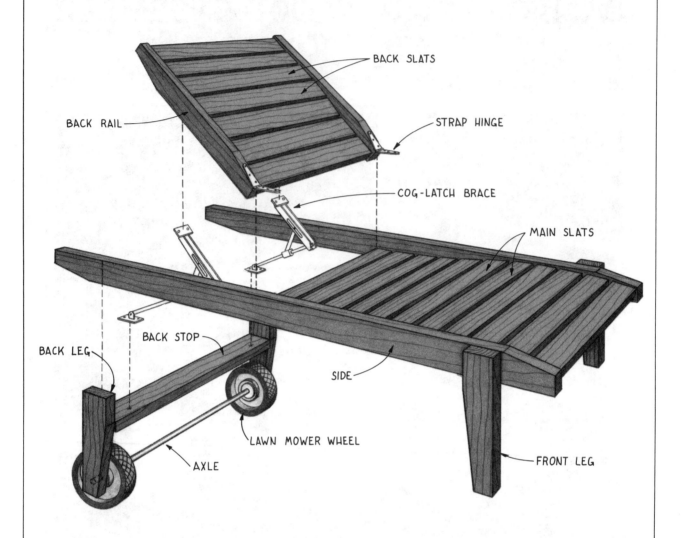

BACK SLATS

BACK RAIL

STRAP HINGE

COG-LATCH BRACE

MAIN SLATS

BACK STOP

BACK LEG

SIDE

LAWN MOWER WHEEL

FRONT LEG

AXLE

SHOPPING LIST

LUMBER

5 pcs. 2 × 4 × 10' construction heart redwood
1 pc. 2 × 4 × 8' construction heart redwood

HARDWARE AND SUPPLIES

80 pcs. #6 × 3" galvanized drywall-type screws
12 pcs. #6 × 1½" galvanized drywall-type screws
8 pcs. #8 × 2½" galvanized drywall-type screws
2 pcs. 7" dia. wheels with rubber tires
1 pc. ½" dia. × 26" steel rod
4 pcs. ½" dia. flat washers
2 pcs. ⅛" dia. cotter pins
2 pcs. 6" strap hinges
1 pr. cog-latch braces*

FINISH

Clear water repellent or clear exterior finish

*Sold by Constantine's, 2050 Eastchester Road, Bronx, NY 10461 (1-800-223-8087 or 212-792-1600) as slant/tilt table hardware (part number FH702). And by The Woodworker's Store, 21801 Industrial Blvd., Rogers, MN 55374 (612-428-2199) as drafting table hardware (part number D5660).

CUTTING LIST

PIECE	NUMBER	THICKNESS	WIDTH	LENGTH	MATERIAL
Sides	2	1½"	3½"	72"	Redwood
Main slats	11	1½"	3½"	21"	Redwood
Back rails	2	1½"	3½"	28"	Redwood
Back slats	7	1½"	3½"	17¾"	Redwood
Back stop	1	1½"	3½"	24"	Redwood
Back legs	2	1½"	3½"	12½"	Redwood
Front legs	2	1½"	3½"	14"	Redwood

CUTTING DIAGRAM

2 x 4 x 10'

| SIDE | BACK RAIL | BACK SLAT |

2 x 4 x 10'

| SIDE | BACK RAIL | BACK SLAT |

2 x 4 x 10'

| MAIN SLAT | MAIN SLAT | MAIN SLAT | MAIN SLAT | MAIN SLAT | BACK LEG |

2 x 4 x 10'

| MAIN SLAT | MAIN SLAT | MAIN SLAT | MAIN SLAT | MAIN SLAT | BACK LEG |

2 x 4 x 10'

| BACK SLAT | BACK SLAT | BACK SLAT | BACK SLAT | BACK SLAT | FRONT LEG | FRONT LEG |

2 x 4 x 8'

| MAIN SLAT | BACK STOP | |

Builder's Notes

A companion project to the chair and settee that opened this chapter, the lounger is constructed with the same materials and uses the same tools and techniques as those earlier projects. If you are building only this project from the ensemble, then by all means read the "Builder's Notes" accompanying the California Redwood Chair and Settee project on page 4.

A few hardware items are unique to the lounger, but you can get most of them at your local hardware store or home center. The wheels, for example, are intended for lawn mowers. The cog-latch braces that support the backrest may be harder to come by, though. There doesn't seem to be a common name used by all retailers. Having obtained our set through the mail, we list two sources (see the "Shopping List").

TOOL LIST

Bar clamps
Centerpunch
Circular saw
Drill
  ⅛" dia. bit (for metal)
  ½" dia. bit
  Countersink bit
  Pilot hole bit
Hacksaw
Hammer
Paintbrush
Router
  ¼" rounding-over bit
  ⅜" V-groove bit

Ruler
Sander(s)
Sandpaper
Sawhorses
Screwdriver
Spring clamps
Tack cloth
Tape measure
Try square

PLAN VIEWS

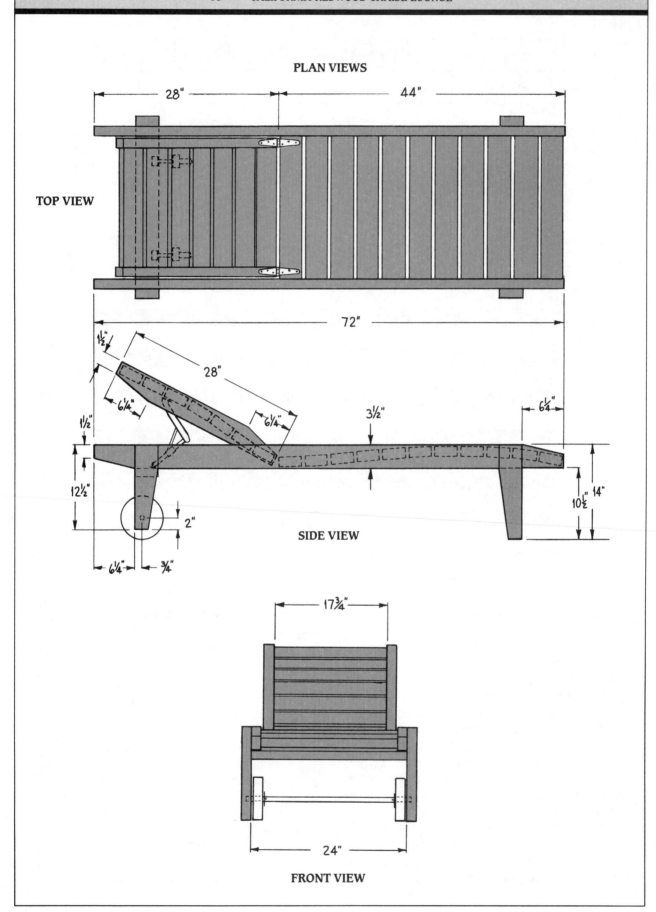

TOP VIEW

SIDE VIEW

FRONT VIEW

1. Cut and assemble the parts for the lounge frame. Cut the sides and main slats for the lounge frame to the lengths specified by the "Cutting List." Lay out and cut the tapers at each end of the side pieces, as shown in the *Side View.* Use a router with a ¼-inch

rounding-over bit to radius all sharp edges.

Assemble the frame by joining the two sides with the end slat and hinge slat.

Establish the contour of the lounge seat next. Stand the partially assembled frame on one side. Hold a strip of plastic laminate or thin plywood on edge against the side. Flex the strip to the desired curve, then, to hold the curve, clamp the strip to the front and hinge slats (use spring clamps). Trace the curve on the side piece. To duplicate the line on the second side, take measurements at several points along the line, then transfer them to the second side. Flex the strip to connect the marks, clamp it, then trace the curve.

That done, fasten the remaining nine slats to the sides with 3-inch screws, following the curve.

To establish the seat contour, flex a strip of plastic laminate or thin plywood until it takes on a curve you like. Use spring clamps to secure the strip to the front and hinge slats, holding the curve so you can trace it with a pencil, marking the side.

2. Make the legs. Cut the front and back legs to length, then taper the sides, as shown in the *Side View.* You can cut the tapers with a portable circular saw if you clamp the leg blanks to a larger piece of scrap. Drill ½-inch-diameter by 1-inch-deep stopped holes into the inside faces of the back legs for the wheel axle, as shown in the *Side View.* Radius all exposed edges of the legs.

Attach the front legs to the lounge frame with 2½-inch screws. When marking the leg positions on the sides, use a try square and pencil to make sure the legs are exactly perpendicular to the sides.

3. Install the wheel assembly. Cut the back stop to fit between the back legs and, with 3-inch screws, fasten it to the bottom edge of the lounge sides.

Cut the 26-inch axle for the wheel assembly from ½-inch-diameter steel rod. As shown, the axle is "captured" by the legs. Likewise, each wheel is captured between a leg and a cotter pin. Drill two ⅛-inch holes in the axle for these cotter pins. The exact positions of the holes are best determined by dry assembling the axle, wheels, and legs. Allow about ¼ inch of side-to-side play for each wheel.

Attach one of the back legs to the lounge side and back stop. Next, insert the axle in the leg hole. Slide on a washer, a wheel, two more washers, the second wheel, and yet another washer. Then, temporarily attach (or clamp) the second leg, capturing the axle and wheels between the legs. Slide the wheels against their respective legs, and mark the axle for the cotter-pin holes.

Remove the axle from the assembly, drill the holes, then reassemble the components. Install the cotter pins in the axle.

To install the axle, fasten one of the back legs to the lounge side and back stop, insert the wheel/axle assembly, then add the other back leg to capture the axle between the two legs.

TIP

Drilling the cotter-pin holes in the steel axle can be done with a hand-held drill just as well as with a drill press. But here are two tips to make the job easier, regardless of the tool you use.

First, make a V-block to cradle the axle. Plow a groove in a scrap of 2 × 4 with a router and a V-groove bit. As shown, the V-block will keep the axle from rolling as you try to drill.

Then use a hammer and centerpunch to dimple the axle where the hole should be. This little depression will be enough to constrain the bit as you start to drill, preventing it from skittering off mark.

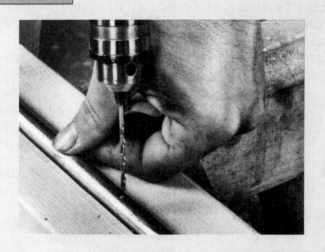

4. Cut and assemble the backrest. Cut the backrest rails and slats to the lengths specified by the "Cutting List," then taper the ends of the back rails, as shown in the *Side View.* With the router and ¼-inch rounding-over bit, radius all the edges that will be exposed.

Using the drawing as a guide, establish the contour formed by the slats on the rails, as you did for the lounge sides. Fasten the back slats to the back rails with 3-inch screws.

---

5. Install the backrest. Center the backrest between the lounge sides, and install the hinges.

The cog-latch braces must now be installed, and

positioning them is a trial-and-error proposition. They must be aligned so that they'll work together without binding *and* allow the back to hinge down perfectly flat.

Begin by propping the back in an upright position. Use 1½-inch screws to attach the top end of each brace to the third back slat from the top (one at each end of the slat, flush against the side rails). Use a C-clamp or short bar clamp to secure the bottom end of each brace to the back stop, as shown. Test the action of the backrest. As necessary, loosen one or both clamps, shift the brace(s), and retighten the clamp(s). When you are satisfied with the action of the braces, fasten the bottom ends with the 1½-inch screws and remove the clamps.

A short bar clamp holds the lower end of the cog-latch brace in place while you test the action. Both braces must work in concert without binding, and to do that, they must be perfectly aligned.

---

6. Apply a finish. Sand the entire piece with fine-grit sandpaper, smoothing any sharp or splintery edges. Apply the clear finish of your choice and let it dry.

That's it—the chaise is ready to be wheeled out to a spot in the sun.

CALIFORNIA REDWOOD ENSEMBLE FOLDING TABLE

This sturdy, 6-foot-long table will hold a smorgasbord of snacks, making your redwood ensemble the focal point of backyard gatherings. If you think it's a bit too big for everyday use on your deck or patio, no problem— just fold up the legs and store it neatly out of the way.

The table complements the ensemble visually. The taper of the leg echoes that of the other pieces of the ensemble. And the joinery of the leg assembly echoes that used for the glider stand.

A bit of ingenuity went into the construction of the table. After testing it, we discarded hardware we had bought that supposedly was designed especially for folding tables; the play in the mechanisms made the table far too wobbly. A pensive stroll through the aisles of the local hardware store led to a different solution: stepladder braces. Like your picnic table, a stepladder in use is laden with precious cargo and must be rock-steady. The braces work perfectly.

SHOPPING LIST

LUMBER

4 pcs. 2 × 4 × 12' construction heart redwood
2 pcs. 2 × 4 × 10' construction heart redwood
1 pc. 2 × 4 × 8' construction heart redwood

HARDWARE AND SUPPLIES

80 pcs. #6 × 2½" galvanized drywall-type screws
24 pcs. #6 × 1¼" galvanized drywall-type screws

HARDWARE AND SUPPLIES—CONTINUED

4 pcs. 6" light-duty T-strap hinges
4 pcs. stepladder braces

FINISH

Clear water repellent or clear exterior finish, if
  desired

CUTTING LIST

PIECE	NUMBER	THICKNESS	WIDTH	LENGTH	MATERIAL
Tabletop slats	8	1½"	3½"	72"	Redwood
Tabletop cleats	3	1½"	3½"	29¼"	Redwood
Brace blocks	4	1½"	3½"	16"	Redwood
Legs	4	1½"	3½"	27"	Redwood
Leg crosspieces	2	1½"	3½"	17¼"	Redwood

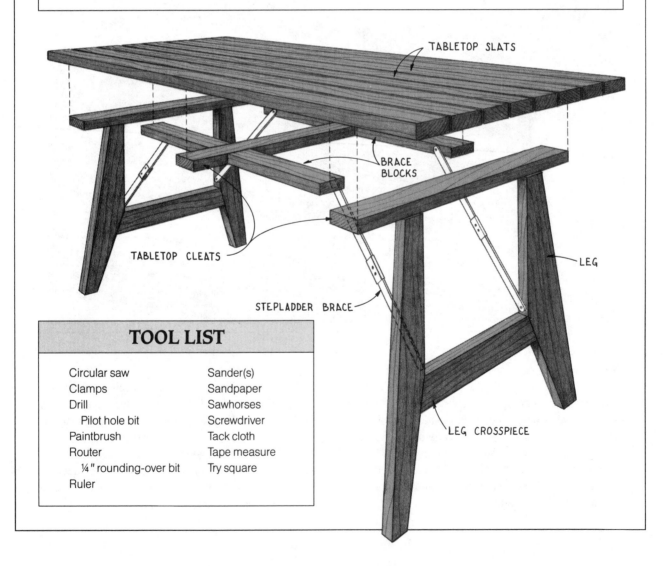

TOOL LIST

Circular saw	Sander(s)
Clamps	Sandpaper
Drill	Sawhorses
Pilot hole bit	Screwdriver
Paintbrush	Tack cloth
Router	Tape measure
¼" rounding-over bit	Try square
Ruler	

PLAN VIEWS

TOP VIEW

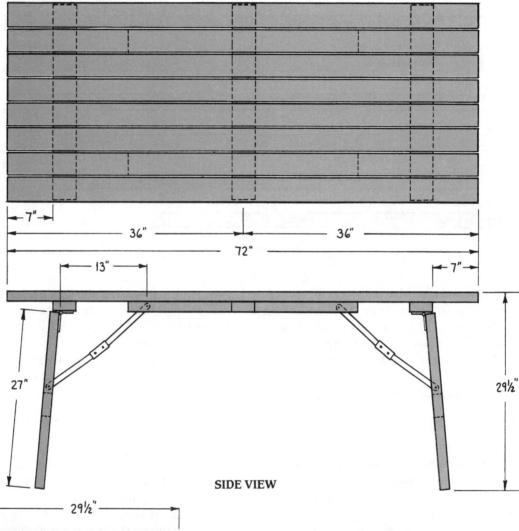

SIDE VIEW

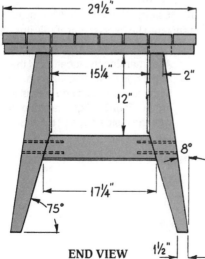

END VIEW

Builder's Notes

A companion project to this chapter's settee, chair, and chaise lounge, the folding table is constructed with the same materials and uses the same tools and techniques as those earlier projects. If you are building only this project from the ensemble, then by all means read the "Builder's Notes" accompanying the California Redwood Chair and Settee project on **page 4**.

One hardware item, the stepladder brace, is unique to the folding table, but you should be able to get it at a well-stocked hardware store or home center.

CUTTING DIAGRAM

2 x 4 x 12'
| TABLETOP SLAT | TABLETOP SLAT |

2 x 4 x 12'
| TABLETOP SLAT | TABLETOP SLAT |

2 x 4 x 12'
| TABLETOP SLAT | TABLETOP SLAT |

2 x 4 x 12'
| TABLETOP SLAT | TABLETOP SLAT |

2 x 4 x 10'
| TABLETOP CLEAT | TABLETOP CLEAT | TABLETOP CLEAT | LEG | |

2 x 4 x 10'
| LEG | LEG | LEG | LEG CROSSPIECE | LEG CROSSPIECE |

2 x 4 x 8'
| BRACE BLOCK | BRACE BLOCK | BRACE BLOCK | BRACE BLOCK | |

1. Cut and assemble the pieces for the top.
Cut the tabletop slats, tabletop cleats, and brace blocks to the lengths specified by the "Cutting List." Using a router and a ¼-inch rounding-over bit, radius all edges of the tabletop slats and the exposed edges of the cleats and brace blocks.

On a workbench or other flat surface, arrange the slats, spacing them evenly to form a top 29½ inches wide. Making sure that the slat ends are perfectly aligned and the tabletop is square, position the cleats across the tabletop, as shown in the *Top View,* and fasten them in place with 2½-inch screws. Use the same size screws to attach the brace blocks to the underside of the tabletop.

2. Lay out and cut the legs. Cut four blanks for the tapered legs to the length specified by the "Cutting List." Lay out the tapered sides and angled ends on one leg, cut the leg out, then use it as a template to lay out the other three. Here's how to lay out that first leg:

• Use a straightedge to extend the line of the inside edge of a brace block across the hinge cleat, as shown in the *Leg Layout.*

• Mark the hinge alignment line on the end tabletop cleat, as shown. The intersection of this line with the

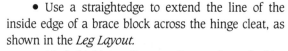

After marking the location of the leg and hinge on a cleat, align the leg blank to the marks and lay out the taper angle. Visually align the straightedge with the inside edge of the brace block beneath.

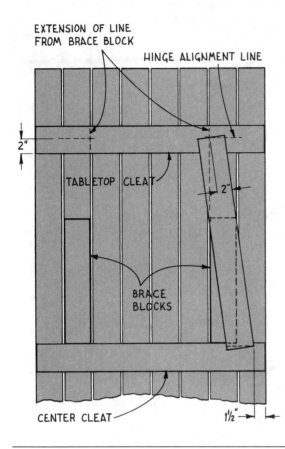

first line is the key alignment point on the end tabletop cleat.

● Measure and mark a line across the center tabletop cleat 1½ inches from the end, as shown.

● At the end of a leg blank, measure and mark 2 inches from the outer edge, as shown.

● Position the leg across the cleats, as shown, with its mark lined up with the alignment point on the end tabletop cleat and its foot flush with the line on the center tabletop cleat.

● Place a straightedge on top of the leg, visually align it with the inside edge of the brace block, and scribe the taper line on the leg. Use the straightedge to mark the top and foot of the leg for cutting; align it visually with the cleats to do this.

● Finally, follow the *End View* to mark the line of the second taper.

Use a circular saw to cut the shape of the leg. For safety's sake, clamp the leg blank to a scrap 2 × 4 supported on sawhorses when you make these cuts. After the other three legs are laid out, cut them in the same way.

---

3. Build the leg assemblies. Cut the leg crosspieces to length, mitering the ends as shown in the *End View.* Assemble both leg sets by drilling pilot holes through the sides of the legs into the ends of the crosspieces, as indicated in the *End View,* then driving 2½-inch screws.

With a router and a rounding-over bit, radius the edges of the two assemblies.

TIP

Here's how to ensure that both leg assemblies will be perfectly flat and will match each other. First, lay out the pieces for the first assembly on a flat bench, and clamp them, not to each other but to the benchtop, as shown. Drill pilot holes and drive the screws. Remove the clamps, lay the pieces for the second assembly on top of the first, and clamp both to the benchtop. You'll see immediately whether or not the assemblies are matched. If they are, install the screws in the second assembly.

4. **Attach the leg assemblies to the tabletop.** Center the strap leaf of the hinges on the ends of the table legs, and fasten the hinges with 1¼-inch screws. Then rest each assembly on the underside of the table-top in its folded position. Clamp the assembly to the tabletop, and drive 1¼-inch screws in the exposed screw holes of the hinge's butt leaf. Now, open up the assembly and drive screws into the remaining holes in the hinge leaf.

To locate the screw holes for the stepladder braces on the brace blocks and legs, use the braces themselves. With both the legs and braces folded, set the braces next to the leg and brace block. Fasten one end to the leg, the other to the brace block. Use 2½-inch screws. Check the action of the leg; it should open easily and completely, as should the braces. If the setup works to your satisfaction, duplicate the procedure to install the other leg assembly.

After attaching the leg assembly to the tabletop, align the folded stepladder brace against the brace block and the leg, and drive the screws to secure it. The position of the second brace must parallel the position of the first for the setup to work smoothly.

5. **Apply a finish.** Lightly sand all surfaces with fine-grit sandpaper and apply the same clear finish you used for the other pieces in the ensemble. If the deeply counterbored screw holes in the legs bother you, you can fill these with a plastic wood dough or putty before sanding and finishing the project.

Now, let's eat outdoors!

ALL-AMERICA PICNIC TABLE

The Backyard's Rugged Standby

This project is called the All-America Picnic Table simply because it's the rugged standby seen all over America—in campgrounds, parks, roadside rests, and at least a few million backyards. The time-honored design has survived for several reasons: It's easy to build with a few basic tools and standard lumber available at any lumberyard, it will seat a family of six comfortably, and it's durable enough to outlast a lifetime of picnics.

Of course, no outdoor furniture book would be complete without one!

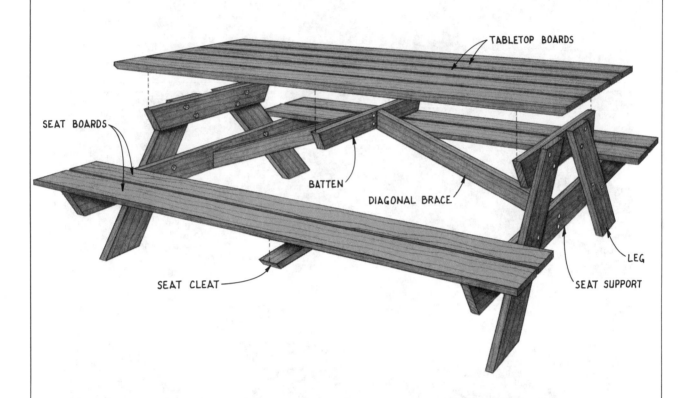

TABLETOP BOARDS

SEAT BOARDS

BATTEN

DIAGONAL BRACE

LEG

SEAT CLEAT

SEAT SUPPORT

SHOPPING LIST

LUMBER

12 pcs. 2 × 6 × 8′ clear all heart redwood
2 pcs. 2 × 4 × 8′ clear all heart redwood

HARDWARE AND SUPPLIES

16 pcs. ¼″ × 3½″ galvanized carriage bolts,
   washers, and nuts
1 box #6 × 2½″ galvanized drywall-type screws
1 box #6 × 3″ galvanized drywall-type screws

FINISH

Clear water repellent or clear exterior finish

CUTTING LIST

PIECE	NUMBER	THICKNESS	WIDTH	LENGTH	MATERIAL
Legs	4	1½″	5½″	33″	2 × 6 redwood
Seat supports	2	1½″	5½″	58½″	2 × 6 redwood
Battens	3	1½″	3½″	28½″	2 × 4 redwood
Diagonal braces	2	1½″	3½″	42″	2 × 4 redwood
Tabletop boards	5	1½″	5½″	96″	2 × 6 redwood
Seat boards	4	1½″	5½″	96″	2 × 6 redwood
Seat cleats	2	1½″	5½″	11″	2 × 6 redwood

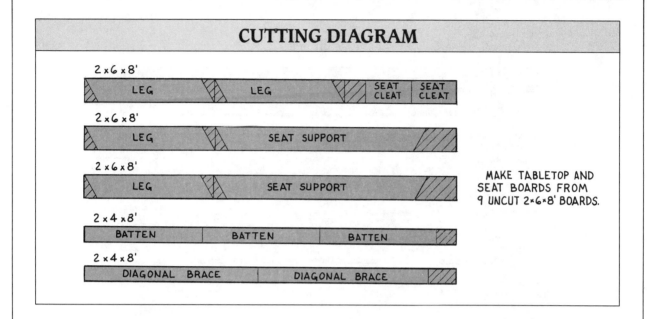

CUTTING DIAGRAM

2 x 6 x 8'
LEG | LEG | SEAT CLEAT | SEAT CLEAT

2 x 6 x 8'
LEG | SEAT SUPPORT

2 x 6 x 8'
LEG | SEAT SUPPORT

2 x 4 x 8'
BATTEN | BATTEN | BATTEN

2 x 4 x 8'
DIAGONAL BRACE | DIAGONAL BRACE

MAKE TABLETOP AND SEAT BOARDS FROM 9 UNCUT 2×6×8' BOARDS.

Builder's Notes

The All-America Picnic Table is an *ideal* project for the complete novice. It is, first of all, imminently practical—you get a piece of furniture you and your family will use for years to come. The materials, though not cheap, are readily available throughout North America. The necessary tools are few and commonplace. (If you really reduce the project to its simplest form, you can get by with a handsaw and a hammer.) And finally, the woodworking processes are basic ones that you'll use again and again as you learn, gain experience, and tackle more demanding projects.

From the drawings and the text, you'll learn how to build a nice, basic picnic table with top-quality lumber and heavy-duty hardware, simple solid joinery, and a few craftsman-like touches, among them the chamfered ends on the tabletop and seat boards, and the hidden fasteners. Following these directions explicitly will require you to purchase premium materials and to have a selection of power tools (and accessories). In the following notes, you'll find specific tips on saving money and time, and simplifying the work.

The table shown is one of dozens crafted by Rodale Press's John Keck for the fair-weather use of the company's employees. Though Keck's picnic tables get fair-weather use, they also get—and withstand—year-round abuse. Because each table is one bulky piece, it's a tough item to store out of the weather. Attesting to the durability of the design and materials is the fact that these tables are left outdoors year-round, in all kinds of weather—spring rains, summer sun, fall frosts, winter snow and ice. Many are five or more years old, and still supporting the heartiest of picnics. And picnickers!

Materials. Perhaps the most obvious thing about the materials is that fully half the boards you buy never get cut. They're used at full length and width in the project.

The next most obvious thing is that we—or at least John Keck—used the premium grade of redwood. Is this *necessary?* Of course not. Buy down a grade. Or select a different wood. But do try to avoid knots and other defects that may undermine the strength of the project. You don't want a seat board to break at a knot and dump Aunt Martha on the ground. (She just might have a litigious reaction.) And select a species that will weather well; your picnic table (like ours) will surely have to withstand the worst that your local climate has to offer.

TOOL LIST

Circular saw	Sander(s)
Clamps	Sandpaper
Drill	Sawhorses
¼ " dia. bit	Screwdriver
⅜" dia. bit	Sliding T-bevel
Long-shank Phillips bit	Tack cloth
Pilot hole bit	Tape measure
Hammer	Try square
Paintbrush	Wrench
Protractor	Yardstick

PLAN VIEWS

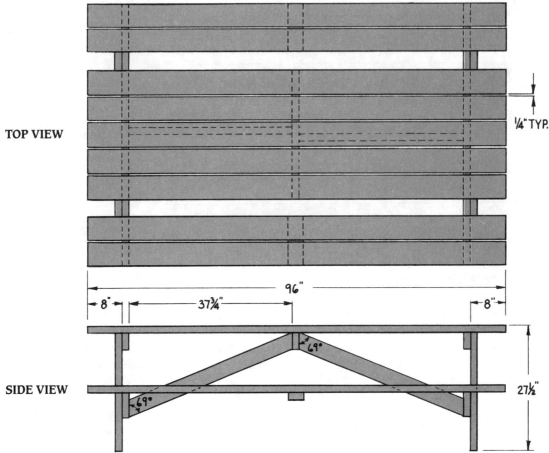

TOP VIEW

¼" TYP.

96"

8" 37¾" 8"

69°

SIDE VIEW

69° 27½"

END VIEW

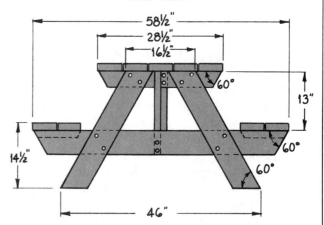

58½"

28½"

16½"

60°

13"

14½"

60°

60°

46"

Think more than once before substituting pressure-treated wood for the redwood in this project, however. Your first thought, of course, will be that this lumber is a lot less expensive. But your second thought ought to be a question: Do I want to eat from a table made of a material that's thoroughly impregnated with an arsenic compound? One that will kill any insects that try to eat it?

If you are willing to paint or varnish your table (and recoat it, say, every other year), you could use construction-grade material—pine, spruce, fir, hemlock, or whatever is commonly used in your area.

Less obvious, perhaps, are the hardware options. The "Shopping List" specifies carriage bolts and drywall-type screws as the fasteners to use. In the original table, almost four dozen lag screws were used to attach the tabletop and seat boards. The drywall-type screws are a less costly choice that is completely satisfactory. Moreover, you can use the screws throughout the project.

Or you can use nails. Not just any nails, of course, but galvanized nails with threaded or ringed shanks. They often are sold under the name "decking nails" or "pressure-treated wood nails."

Tools and techniques. The woodworking tools you have and the techniques you use are always entwined. The picnic table shown was built using shop tools: a radial arm saw to chamfer the seat and tabletop boards, and a drill press to make the pilot holes and counterbores in the battens and seat supports. The directions below outline how to build the table using portable tools exclusively—a circular saw and a ⅜-inch power drill. But the cutting necessary is so minimal that you can use a handsaw to do it.

Laying out the miters for the legs, braces, and seat supports can be done in a variety of ways. Use a protractor to set a sliding T-bevel, then scribe along the bevel's blade to mark the wood. With a chop saw or radial arm saw at your disposal, you don't have to mark the lumber at all; just set the saw and cut. To aid the woodworker using a circular saw, several companies make relatively inexpensive guides—saw protractors and so-called speed squares. You clench the guide to the wood with one hand, and slide the saw along it with the other. You'll find the guides at most home centers and hardware stores.

Making all the pilot holes and counterbores is one of the biggest parts of this project. As noted, this work was originally done on a drill press. There's no reason, though, why it can't be done with a hand-held power drill. The point of the approach is to conceal the fasteners, both for the aesthetic benefit and to avoid providing water with spots to accumulate and penetrate, leading to rot.

But if *really* quick-and-easy is what you want, you can skip the counterboring and simply drive screws or nails through the tabletop boards into the battens. The heads will be visible, but the work will be expedited and the tool requirements minimized.

Finish. The picnic table shown doesn't have a finish. Redwood is as resistant to the effects of moisture as a wood can be. The heart of redwood is naturally resistant to the growth of rot-producing fungi. Moreover, redwood is very light (not dense). Thus, the table won't rot, and it is relatively resistant to cupping and splitting.

After a year or two in the sun, the redwood's natural color slowly shifts to a silvery-gray. You can try to fight this color shift with finishes containing ultraviolet absorbers (UVAs). How successful you will be depends upon how diligent you are at keeping the table's finish fresh.

---

1. Cut the legs, seat supports, and battens.

Cut these pieces to the lengths specified by the "Cutting List." Then miter the ends of each piece at the angles indicated in the *End View.*

Drill and counterbore pilot holes in each batten. Since you eventually will drive two 3-inch screws through each batten into each tabletop board, a total of ten are needed. Lay out the holes, as shown in the *Batten Layout.*

Drill the counterbores first, making each ⅜ inch in diameter by 1¾ inches deep. Don't bore them too deep, or you'll risk having screws emerge through the tabletop during assembly. Next, drill pilot holes for the screws; if your bit isn't long enough to completely penetrate the batten—and it probably won't be—make them as deep as you can.

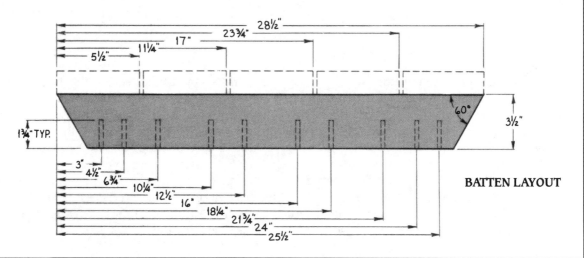

BATTEN LAYOUT

You can mark the miters with a sliding T-bevel and protractor. Or, you can use a saw protractor. This simple device can guide any miter up to 60 degrees. With it, you simply mark the length of your piece with a tape measure, then hold the protractor or square tightly to the stock at the appropriate angle. With the base shoe of your saw against the guide, align the blade with the mark and make the cut.

To simplify drilling the counterbores, mark the proper depth on the drill bit by wrapping tape around it, leaving a little flag. When the flag brushes the batten's surface, the counterbore is just deep enough.

2. **Assemble the leg units.** Begin the assembly process by laying a batten and a seat support on a flat surface and arranging the legs on top of them, as shown in the *End View.* Clamp the legs in place and drill ¼-inch-diameter holes for the carriage bolts that will hold the parts together. Two bolts in each joint should be sufficient. Insert the bolts into the legs and through the batten or support, then add a washer and nut. Tighten it down.

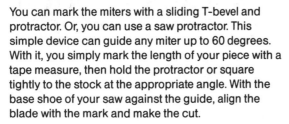

TIP

You can save a little hardware money by fastening the leg assemblies with 2½-inch galvanized drywall-type screws, rather than carriage bolts. Drive four screws into each joint.

3. **Assemble the tabletop.** When you buy them, the five tabletop boards should be the correct length. Select the best side of each, and arrange them on your sawhorses or a flat surface with the good side down.

Rest the center batten (the one not used when you assembled the legs) on the tabletop boards, centering it as shown in the *Top View.* Space the top boards evenly, so the two outside top boards are flush with the end of the batten. An easy way to do this is to use scraps of

¼-inch plywood as spacers between the boards.

Drive 3-inch screws through the batten into the tabletop boards. If you use a drill-driver, you'll need a long-shanked Phillips bit (Black & Decker sells bits in lengths up to 6 inches). Don't be too aggressive when driving the screws; redwood is pretty soft, and the torque of a drill-driver can bury the screws to the degree that their points will emerge through the tabletop boards. (If your counterbores prove to be too deep, simply substitute shorter screws.)

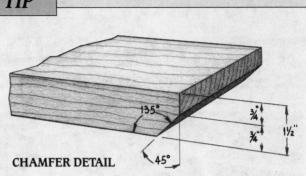
4. **Attach the leg assemblies to the tabletop.** Mark the positions of the leg assemblies across the tabletop boards. Support one assembly in an upright position (have a helper do this, or clamp the assembly to the tabletop), then drive 3-inch screws through the battens into the tabletop boards. Attach the second leg assembly in the same manner.

5. **Cut and install the diagonal braces.** Cut the diagonal braces to length, and miter the ends, as shown in the *Side View.* With the table still upside down, attach the diagonal braces to the seat supports and center batten with 3-inch screws, driving two screws at each joint.

6. **Install the seat boards.** With the table still upside down, drill pilot holes and 3¾-inch-deep counterbores through the bottom edges of the seat supports for the screws that attach the seat boards. Position the holes, as shown in the *Seat Support Detail.*

Get some help to turn the table onto its feet; if you can stand it on sawhorses, it will make the seat installation a little easier. Position the seat boards on the supports and clamp them. Then drive 3-inch screws through the supports into the seat boards.

Trim the seat cleats as necessary, and bevel their ends. Attach them to the bottom of the seat boards, midway between the seat supports. Use the 2½-inch screws.

SEAT SUPPORT DETAIL

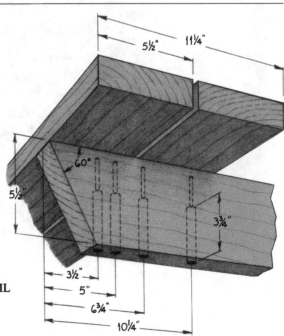

7. **Apply a finish.** After a once-over with a finish sander, apply a clear exterior finish such as CWF, or a water repellent such as Thompson's Water Seal.

SOUTHERN PINE TABLE AND BENCHES

Simply Elegant for Deck or Patio

This smart pine table and bench set, with its sleek tapered legs, mitered corners, and diagonal board top, is a fine example of such simple elegance. The clean lines and finished appearance will add just the right touch of class to your deck or patio. But don't let the light, somewhat delicate look of the table and benches fool you—they're plenty sturdy. The set will seat six adults comfortably with plenty of elbow room.

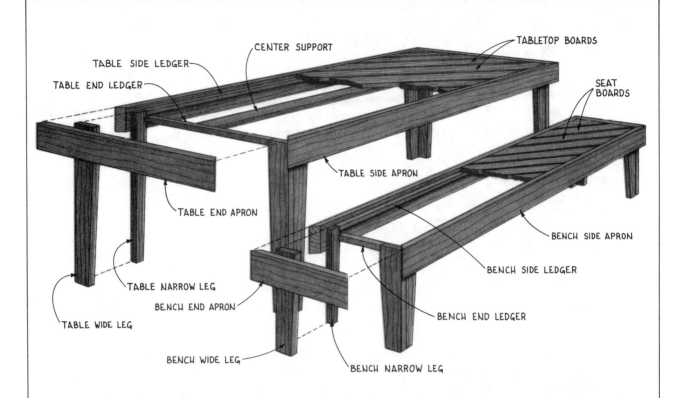

CENTER SUPPORT
TABLETOP BOARDS
TABLE SIDE LEDGER
TABLE END LEDGER
SEAT BOARDS
TABLE SIDE APRON
TABLE END APRON
BENCH SIDE APRON
TABLE NARROW LEG
BENCH SIDE LEDGER
BENCH END APRON
TABLE WIDE LEG
BENCH END LEDGER
BENCH WIDE LEG
BENCH NARROW LEG

SHOPPING LIST

LUMBER

2 pcs. 5/4 × 4 × 10' #2 pine
2 pcs. 5/4 × 3 × 10' #2 pine
4 pcs. 5/4 × 6 × 12' #2 pine
12 pcs. 1 × 4 × 8' #2 pine

HARDWARE AND SUPPLIES

1 box #6 × 2" galvanized drywall-type screws
3 boxes #6 × 1½" galvanized drywall-type screws
2 tubes construction adhesive, 10-oz. size

FINISH

Semitransparent preservative stain

Builder's Notes

This is an excellent project for the beginning woodworker. It's built with lumber that's basic stock at any good lumberyard, and the essential tools will be in a basic tool kit. The required cutting and the joinery techniques specified are basic and easily mastered. A shop isn't necessary; you can cut the parts and assemble them in your yard.

Materials. On the "Shopping List," we've included enough lumber and hardware to build the table and two benches.

TOOL LIST

Bar clamps	Sander(s)
Caulking gun	Sandpaper
Circular saw	Saw for ripping
Drill	Sawhorses
Phillips bit	Screwdriver
Pilot hole bit	Tack cloth
Hammer	Tape measure
Paintbrush	Yardstick
Router	
¼" rounding-over bit	

CUTTING LIST

PIECE	NUMBER	THICKNESS	WIDTH	LENGTH	MATERIAL
Table					
Wide legs*	4	1⅛"	3½"	28¼"	5/4 × 4
Narrow legs*	4	1⅛"	2½"	28¼"	5/4 × 3
End aprons	2	1⅛"	4½"	36"	5/4 × 6
Side aprons	2	1⅛"	4½"	72"	5/4 × 6
End ledgers	2	¾"	1⅛"	26¾"	5/4†
Side ledgers	2	¾"	1⅛"	62½"	5/4†
Center support	1	¾"	3½"	67½"	1 × 4
Tabletop boards	19	¾"	3½"	various‡	1 × 4
Benches					
Wide legs*	8	1⅛"	3½"	14¾"	5/4 × 4
Narrow legs*	8	1⅛"	2½"	14¾'	5/4 × 3
End aprons	4	1⅛"	4½"	16"	5/4 × 6
Side aprons	4	1⅛"	4½"	72"	5/4 × 6
End ledgers	4	¾"	1⅛"	6½"	5/4†
Side ledgers	4	¾"	1⅛"	62½"	5/4†
Seat boards	16	¾"	3½"	various§	1 × 4

*Dimensions of piece before tapers are cut
†Use scrap ripped from apron piece.
‡Approx. 60 lineal feet; cut to fit.
§Approx. 50 lineal feet; cut to fit.

CUTTING DIAGRAM

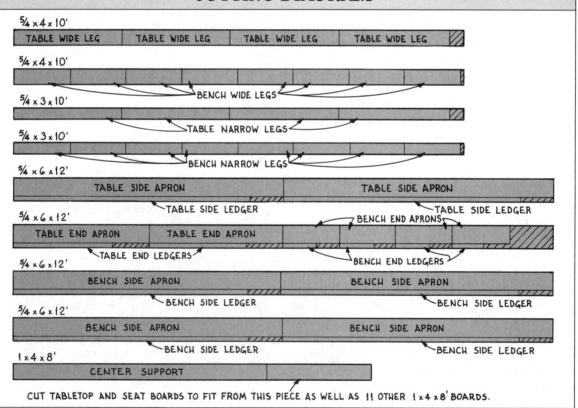

CUT TABLETOP AND SEAT BOARDS TO FIT FROM THIS PIECE AS WELL AS 11 OTHER 1 x 4 x 8' BOARDS.

TABLE PLAN VIEWS

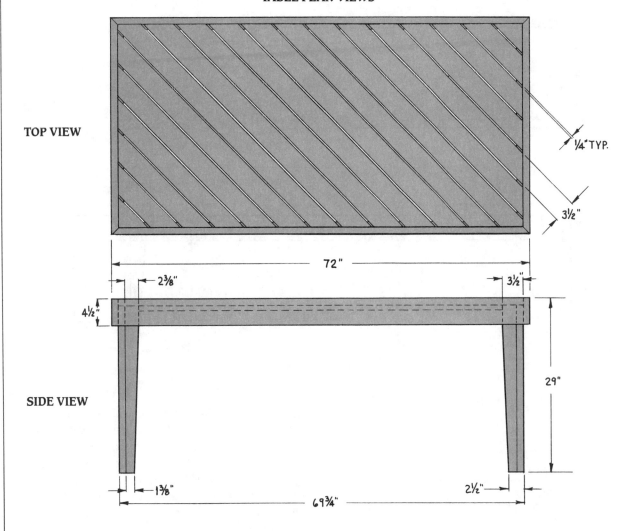

TOP VIEW

¼" TYP.

3½"

72"

2⅜"   3½"

4½"

29"

SIDE VIEW

1⅜"   2½"

69¾"

Five-quarter (5/4) stock measures approximately 1⅛ inches. The pine we used is generally available in the same widths and lengths as the more familiar 1-by material. Number 2 grade is perfectly suitable for this project. (A price check at your local lumberyard probably will reveal that a clear grade costs double—or even more—what the number 2 grade does.)

We used screws—the galvanized drywall-type—and construction adhesive to assemble both the table and the benches. Screws cost more than nails, and considering the number used in this project, you almost *need* a drill-driver to install them. (In fact, the drywall-type screws are designed to be power-driven.) But screws hold better: They can be tightened if time, wood movement, and hard use loosens them, and the process of installing them isn't likely to whack the parts you are joining out of alignment.

END VIEW

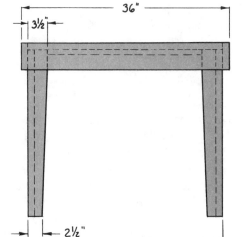

36"

3½"

2½"

33¾"

BENCH PLAN VIEWS

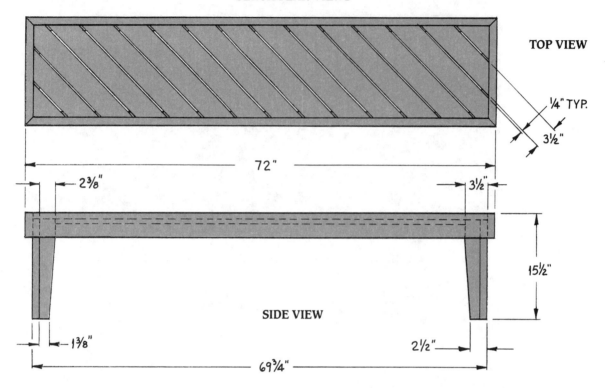

TOP VIEW

¼" TYP.

3½"

72"

2⅜"

3½"

15½"

SIDE VIEW

1⅜"

2½"

69¾"

END VIEW

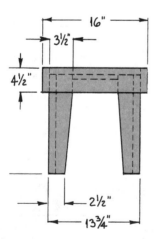

16"

3½"

4½"

2½"

13¾"

Construction adhesive is packaged in tubes like caulk. You need a caulking gun to apply it. Buy a water-proof adhesive that's suitable for bonding wood to wood. When applying it, run a *narrow* bead along *one* of the pieces to be joined; otherwise, any excess glue may show on the finished piece.

Tools and techniques. The construction of this set is easily accomplished with hand tools and two portable power tools—a drill and a circular saw. While you do have to make a lot of miter cuts and some taper cuts, you can make all of them with a circular saw. You do have to rip the aprons to width, which is most easily done on a table saw. But even the rip can safely and effectively be done with a circular saw. Equipping the saw with a combination blade will permit you to make all the rips, miter cuts, taper cuts, and crosscuts without swapping blades.

Finish. To finish the set, we chose a gray semi-transparent preservative stain to give a weathered appearance. Semitransparent stains are only moderately pigmented and thus do not totally hide the wood grain. They penetrate the wood surface, are porous, but do not form a surface film like paints. As a result, they will not blister or peel, even if moisture moves through the wood. Penetrating stains are oil-based or alkyd-based (synthetic oil), and some may contain a fungicide. Semitransparent stains are not inherently resistant to moisture, but some have a water repellent such as paraffin. Moderately pigmented latex stains also are available, but they do not penetrate the wood surfaces as do the oil-based stains.

Stains come in an ever-increasing variety of colors, but not as many as paint or solid-color stains. White is not available. We used a light gray color.

1. **Cut and assemble the table legs.** Cut and taper the eight pieces necessary to form the legs; follow the dimensions in the *Table Plan Views.* With a router and a ¼″ rounding-over bit, radius each tapered side.

To form the legs, join a narrow leg piece to a wide leg piece using construction adhesive and 2-inch screws. Note in the *Table Side View* and *Table End View* that the wide leg piece is always oriented to adjoin the table's end apron. To achieve this, you must assemble the legs in mirror-image pairs. Don't make all four legs the same. After assembling the legs, radius the outside corner formed by the two leg pieces.

To assemble a leg, glue and screw a narrow leg to a wide one. Run a bead of construction adhesive on the wide leg, then press the narrow leg in place. Drill pilot holes, then drive the screws. Three screws per leg are sufficient.

TIP

To make the tapered leg pieces safely with a circular saw, try cutting the tapers *before* sawing the piece to length.

You'll be cutting four legs from a 10-foot length of 5/4 stock. Rest the board across two sawhorses. Mark the crosscut for the first leg, then lay out the taper with the narrowest part at the butt end of the board. Lay out a second leg piece at the opposite end of the same board. With the circular saw, cut the tapers for both pieces, then crosscut them from the board. Lay out two more legs on the remaining stock, then cut them out.

2. **Cut and assemble the aprons.** From the 5/4 × 6 stock, rip the side and end aprons to the width specified by the "Cutting List." Save the waste from the rips to make the side and end ledgers.

The four apron pieces are joined to each other with end miter joints. To prepare the aprons, set your portable circular saw to cut a 45-degree bevel, then use it to crosscut the aprons to length. Be sure to orient the bevel cuts as shown in the *Table Top View.*

Radius the edges (but not the ends) of the apron pieces with the router and a ¼-inch rounding-over bit. Arrange the apron pieces on your bench, and assemble them into a frame with construction adhesive and 2-inch screws. At each joint, you should drive two screws through the side apron into the end apron, as well as two through the end apron into the side apron. To anchor the aprons during assembly, use bar clamps, applying one jaw to the top edge of the apron and the other to the underside of the work surface. A scrap of wood between the jaw and the apron will protect the workpiece.

3. **Attach the legs to the aprons.** First, lay out and cut the two triangular corner pieces for the tabletop. With the apron assembly upside down on your bench, slip this piece under each leg at each corner to position the legs while you attach them to the apron assembly. Attach the legs to the aprons with construction adhesive and 1½-inch screws.

With the apron assembly clamped to the workbench and the triangular corner piece used as a spacer, apply construction adhesive and fit the leg in place. Drive a couple of screws through each leg piece into the apron assembly.

4. **Cut and attach the ledgers.** Use the scrap ripped from the aprons to make the ledgers. Cut two end ledgers and two side ledgers to the dimensions specified by the "Cutting List."

Apply a bead of construction adhesive to each ledger, press the ledger in place, and drive several 1¼-inch screws through the ledger into the apron. Align the top surface of each ledger flush with the top of the legs, as shown in the *Table Side View* and *Table End View*, so the tabletop boards will be flush with the top edge of the aprons.

5. **Cut and attach the tabletop boards and center support.** Measure, mark, and cut the diagonal top boards to fit inside the frame formed by the aprons. The best way to do this is to start at diagonally opposite corners with the triangular pieces, setting them loosely in place. Then measure, cut, and loose-fit successive boards, leaving a ¼-inch space between each. The process will ensure you get a uniform layout. The last board to be cut will be the middle one; if it needs to be wider or narrower than the others to close the last gap it won't throw off the symmetry of the top.

When all the boards are cut and fitted, number them with a pencil and remove them from the frame. With a router and a ¼-inch rounding-over bit, radius the top edges of the boards, including the mitered ends.

To install the tabletop boards, start at the corners and work toward the middle. After you have four boards installed at each corner, attach the center support to the boards with screws and adhesive. The center support is attached only to the boards, not to the ledgers; it serves merely to tie the boards together. Install the remaining boards, gluing and screwing them to the ledgers and center support from underneath.

Install the tabletop boards with the table standing on its legs. Apply a short bead of adhesive to a board, press the board in place, then drill pilot holes and drive two galvanized 1¼-inch screws through the ledger into the board. The center support can be installed as soon as you get four boards installed at each end.

6. Cut and assemble the bench frames. The benches are made exactly the way the table is made. The dimensions are different, of course, and they have no center supports. Otherwise, they are the same.

Cut the bench legs to the dimensions specified by the "Cutting List." Repeat the process described in step 1 of cutting the tapers, then crosscutting the legs to length. Rip the aprons to width, saving the waste for the ledgers.

As you crosscut the aprons to length, bevel the ends for end miter joints.

Assemble the legs and the apron framework with construction adhesive and 2-inch screws. Cut the triangular corner pieces for the bench seats, and use them as spacers in positioning the legs for attachment to the apron frames. Use the adhesive and 1¼-inch screws to attach the legs.

7. Cut and install the seat boards. This operation is also a repeat of the corresponding table-construction step. Start at diagonally opposite corners, setting the triangular pieces loosely in place. Measure, cut, and loose-fit successive seat boards, leaving a ¼-inch space between each. After all the boards are cut, radius the top edges of the boards, including the mitered ends, with a router and a ¼-inch rounding-over bit.

Start installing the seat boards at the corners of the benches and work toward the middle. Apply a short bead of adhesive to a seat board, press it in place, then drill pilot holes and drive two 1¼-inch screws through the ledger into the seat board.

8. Apply a finish. Sand the table and benches, then apply a semitransparent preservative stain. For a more finished look, you can cover the exposed screw heads with wood putty prior to staining.

PICNIC TABLE AND BENCHES IN THE ROUND

A Round Table to Serve Summer's Conversations

The prototypical picnic table—the granddaddy of them all—is the familiar redwood-colored one with "sawbuck" 2 × 4 legs and 2 × 6 plank top. It has a couple of matching benches with the same redwood color, sawbuck legs, and plank seats. And why shouldn't it be the prototype? Easy to make, it is nevertheless sturdy and durable. Inexpensive, it looks "right" in a wooded glade, on a grassy terrace, or on a sunny deck.

Because an outdoor furniture book would be incomplete without one, here it is. Don't recognize it? That's because it's round. Making it round doesn't make it any more difficult to build, but roundness enhances its role

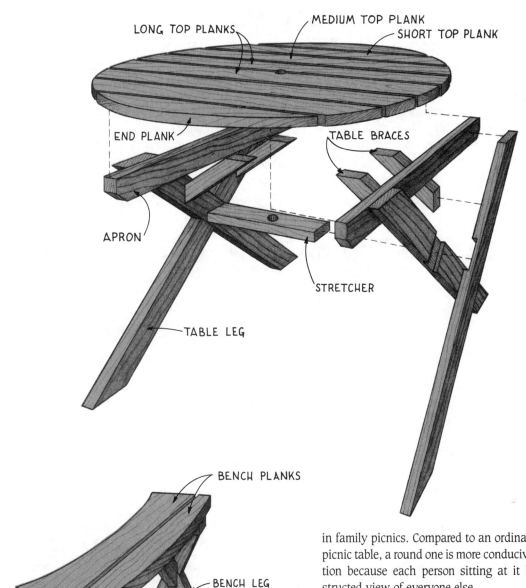

LONG TOP PLANKS

MEDIUM TOP PLANK

SHORT TOP PLANK

END PLANK

TABLE BRACES

APRON

STRETCHER

TABLE LEG

BENCH PLANKS

BENCH LEG

BENCH BRACE

CLEAT

in family picnics. Compared to an ordinary rectangular picnic table, a round one is more conducive to conversation because each person sitting at it has an unobstructed view of everyone else.

For seating, there are curved benches that each seat two. The table itself most comfortably accommodates four adults but will handle six place settings if you don't put too many other goodies on it.

Builder's Notes

You'll find that the project will go faster if you lay out and cut the parts for the table and the benches at the same time, then assemble each separately. The shopping and cutting lists assume you'll be making the table and three curved benches.

Materials. Any number of woods can be used to construct this table and benches. Woods that are either

SHOPPING LIST

LUMBER

1 pc. 2 × 6 × 8′ construction-grade lumber
2 pcs. 2 × 6 × 10′ construction-grade lumber
1 pc. 2 × 4 × 8′ construction-grade lumber
1 pc. 2 × 4 × 10′ construction-grade lumber
1 pc. 2 × 3 × 12′ construction-grade lumber
1 pc. 5/4 × 6 × 10′ #2 pine
2 pcs. 5/4 × 6 × 12′ #2 pine

HARDWARE AND SUPPLIES

8 pcs. ⅜″ × 3½″ galvanized carriage bolts,
     washers, and nuts
4 pcs. ⅜″ × 4″ lag screws and washers
16 pcs. #12 × 2½″ flathead wood screws
1 lb. 10d spiral decking nails
1 box #6 × 2″ galvanized drywall-type screws
1 box #6 × 2½″ galvanized drywall-type screws

FINISH

Exterior paint or clear exterior finish of your choice
     for all pieces

CUTTING LIST

PIECE	NUMBER	THICKNESS	WIDTH	LENGTH	MATERIAL
Long top planks	2	1½″	5½″	45¾″	2 × 6
Medium top planks	2	1½″	5½″	44¾″	2 × 6
Short top planks	2	1½″	5½″	40″	2 × 6
End planks	2	1½″	5½″	30½″	2 × 6
Aprons	2	1½″	2½″	41¾″	2 × 3
Table legs	4	1½″	3½″	44¼″	2 × 4
Stretcher	1	1½″	3½″	18⅛″	2 × 4
Table braces	4	1½″	2⅜″	12½″	2 × 3
Bench planks	6	1¹⁄₁₆″	5½″	36″	5/4 × 6 pine
Bench legs	12	1¹⁄₁₆″	2½″	16¼″	5/4 × 6 pine
Bench braces	6	1¹⁄₁₆″	2½″	11″	5/4 × 6 pine
Cleats	6	1¹⁄₁₆″	2½″	9″	5/4 × 6 pine

naturally or artificially rot resistant are the obvious choices.

Redwood is traditional for picnic tables, and it has several advantages. It looks attractive, and it is naturally rot resistant. Equally important, it is not as dense as other woods (like hardwood or pressure-treated wood). A table or bench made of it won't be too heavy. The top and bench planks will resist cupping and cracking. Moreover, redwood is readily available in both the 2-by and 5/4 (five-quarter) stock specified for this project.

Pressure-treated wood is (mostly) southern yellow pine. It is fairly dense, and as such is prone to cupping and cracking. It will also yield a heavy piece of furniture. And it has the disadvantage of being laden with chromated copper arsenate, which poisons any fungi or insects that try to consume the wood. Is this a good choice for a picnic table?

We chose common construction-grade lumber for the table, pine for the benches. The exact wood you get

TOOL LIST

Bar clamps	Saber saw
Clamps	Sander(s)
Drill	Sandpaper
⅜″ bit	Saw for crosscutting
Countersink bit	Saw for ripping
Pilot hole bit	Sawhorses
Hammer	Screwdriver
Hole saw, 1¾″ dia.	Tack cloth
Paintbrush	Tape measure
Power miter saw	Trammel
Radial arm saw	Try square
Dado set	Wrench
Rasp	Yardstick
Router	
¼″ rounding-over bit	

CUTTING DIAGRAM

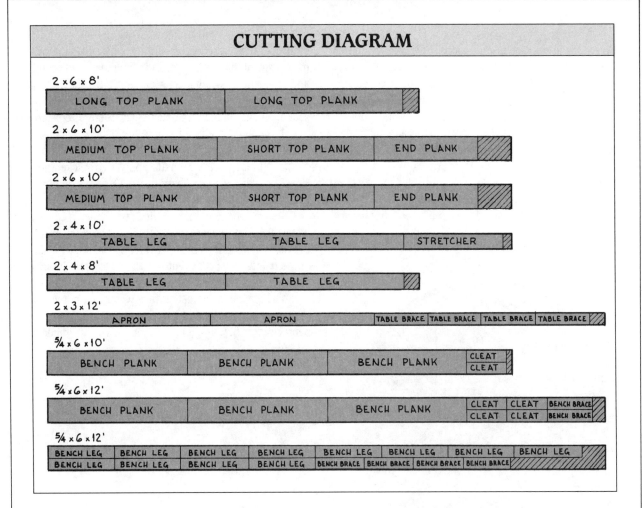

2 × 6 × 8'

| LONG TOP PLANK | LONG TOP PLANK | |

2 × 6 × 10'

| MEDIUM TOP PLANK | SHORT TOP PLANK | END PLANK | |

2 × 6 × 10'

| MEDIUM TOP PLANK | SHORT TOP PLANK | END PLANK | |

2 × 4 × 10'

| TABLE LEG | TABLE LEG | STRETCHER | |

2 × 4 × 8'

| TABLE LEG | TABLE LEG | |

2 × 3 × 12'

| APRON | APRON | TABLE BRACE | TABLE BRACE | TABLE BRACE | TABLE BRACE | |

5/4 × 6 × 10'

| BENCH PLANK | BENCH PLANK | BENCH PLANK | CLEAT / CLEAT |

5/4 × 6 × 12'

| BENCH PLANK | BENCH PLANK | BENCH PLANK | CLEAT / CLEAT | CLEAT / CLEAT | BENCH BRACE / BENCH BRACE |

5/4 × 6 × 12'

| BENCH LEG | BENCH LEG | BENCH LEG | BENCH LEG | BENCH LEG | BENCH LEG | BENCH LEG | BENCH LEG |
| BENCH LEG | BENCH LEG | BENCH LEG | BENCH LEG | BENCH BRACE | BENCH BRACE | BENCH BRACE | BENCH BRACE |

when you order 2-by lumber may vary—it will probably be hemlock, fir, or spruce. Any of these will be satisfactory. A thorough finishing job is essential, of course.

The leg assembly for the table is made from 2 × 4s; the top, 2 × 6s. Because 2-by lumber (1½ inches thick) would have made the benches too bulky, we built them from 5/4 stock, which measures 1 1/16 inches thick. Be picky when you select the wood—you're going to sit and eat on those boards. You want them to be fairly clear and free of defects.

All fasteners should be galvanized or otherwise weather-resistant. For the benches, we used galvanized drywall-type screws because they drive easier than flat-head wood screws when using a power screwdriver or drill-driver. Drill pilot holes for all screws.

Tools and techniques. The essential tools for this project are on the "Tool List." The ideal crosscutting tool for this project is the power miter saw, which makes fast, accurate miters; there are a lot of them to cut. You'll also need a saber saw to make curved cuts.

The umbrella hole in the table was made on a drill press fitted with a 1¾-inch-diameter hole saw. But the hole saw can be chucked in a ½-inch portable drill for the operation (and some hole saws will fit a ⅜-inch chuck), so the drill press is not essential.

To draw the arcs for the tabletop and benchtops, you *can* make a simple string compass, using a non-stretching mason's twine. Attach one end of the twine to a nail for a pivot point, the other end to a pencil. We used a trammel, however. We made it up using commercial trammel points and a 5-foot-long strip of wood about the width and thickness of a yardstick. The trammel is a little bit easier for a lone woodworker to manipulate.

Finish. As noted above, a durable outdoor finish is essential to the longevity of your picnic table and benches (or stools), especially if you follow our lead and build it of pine or fir. What you need in a finish is something that tempers the effects of sunlight and moisture on the wood.

Moisture affects wood several ways. It is a critical requirement for the growth of the fungi that rot wood. When it soaks into wood, it causes it to swell. As it migrates out of the wood, it causes the wood to shrink.

This cyclical expansion and contraction produces tensions within the wood that are released when the wood cups, cracks, splits, and checks. In general, the denser the wood, the more prone it is to cracking and cupping.

Sunlight damages wood in a process called photodegradation. The ultraviolet rays of the sun turn the wood gray and cause its exposed surfaces to disintegrate. In most applications, this surface erosion is too slow to worry about—about ¼ inch per century for softwoods, even less for dense hardwoods.

Paint does the best overall job of protecting wood outdoors. It is best for preventing erosion. Paint has more pigment than solid-color and semitransparent stains, and pigment is what blocks out the sun's degrading effects. Also, paint forms a film on the wood (instead of soaking in, as stain does), which further retards erosion.

In general, oil-based paints are more resistant to moisture than latex paints. The advantage of latex paints is that they are easier to apply, dry quicker, and clean up with water. Cleanup for oil paints requires mineral spirits.

Before brushing on our paint, we applied a coat of water-repellent preservative. Applied before priming, the water-repellent preservative greatly prolongs the life of the paint. Water-repellent preservatives are mixtures of petroleum solvents, paraffin, resins, or drying oils that seal the wood against surface water (but not water vapor), and preservatives like copper naphthenate and pentachlorophenol that prevent the growth of mildew and fungi.

TABLE PLAN VIEWS

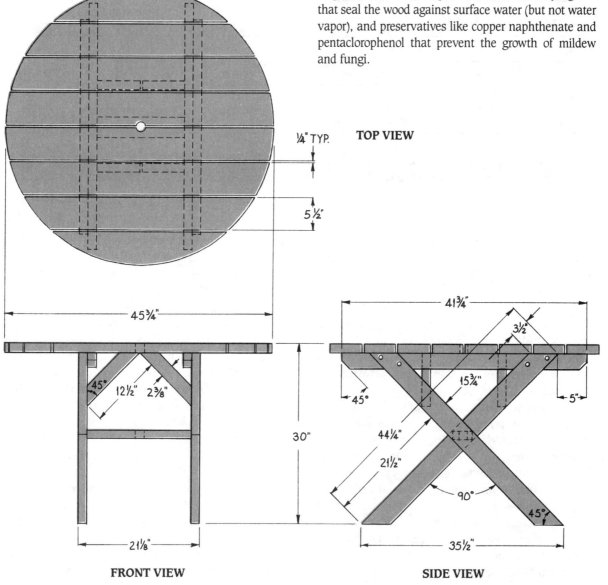

TOP VIEW

FRONT VIEW

SIDE VIEW

1. Cut the parts to size. Rip and crosscut all the parts for the table and benches to the sizes specified by the "Cutting List."

Miter the ends of the table legs and braces at 45 degrees, as shown in the *Table Front View* and the *Table Side View.* Miter the ends of the bench legs at 65 degrees, the bench braces at 45 degrees.

Chamfer the ends of the table aprons to remove sharp corners on which you could bump your legs.

TIP

To avoid mixing up the table parts and bench parts, make neat stacks of cut stock, so you know which parts belong to which piece of furniture. It also helps to label each part or stack of identical parts; if you don't want to spend extra time sanding off pencil marks, though, write the name of each part on a Post-it note and attach it to the part.

The power miter saw is the optimal tool for mitering the table and bench legs. The workpiece remains stationary, while the motor and blade arc in a chopping motion— hence the popular name, chop saw—to make the cut. A stop block—we used a small hand screw clamped on the fence—allows you to cut lengths of stock into parts of uniform length and with the proper miters, quickly and without repetitive layout work.

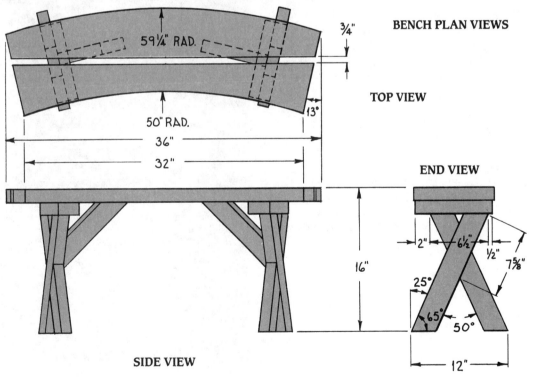

BENCH PLAN VIEWS

59¼" RAD.

¾"

TOP VIEW

50" RAD.

36"

32"

13°

END VIEW

16"

2" 6½" ½"

7⅝"

25°

65° 50°

12"

SIDE VIEW

2. Lay out and cut the lap joints in the legs. The table legs intersect at 90 degrees; the bench legs intersect at 50 degrees. Working with the dimensions shown in the *Table Side View* and *Bench End View,* mark the positions of the lap joints on each set of legs for the table and benches.

To cut the lap joints, you can fit a radial arm saw or table saw with a dado set and make several passes to remove the material between the marked lines. If you don't have a dado set, you can make a series of parallel cuts (about ¼ inch apart) with your saw, then chisel out the waste. Set the depth of the blade to make cuts exactly half the thickness of the stock.

Note: From this point on, steps for assembling the table and benches will be listed separately. You'll probably find it easier to work on the benches until you get them completely assembled, then do the table. After assembly, you can sand and finish all the pieces at one time.

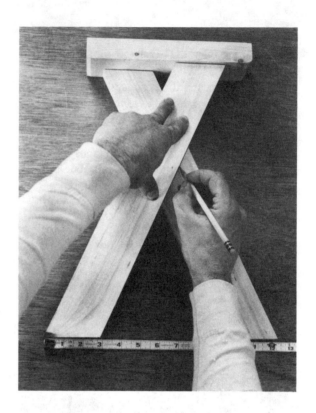

To lay out the lap joints on the legs, lay one leg atop the other, with the top ends flush against a straightedge (for the bench legs, you can use one of the cleats as a straightedge, as shown here). Use a tape measure to set the distance between the bottom ends of the legs to determine the layout position.

3. Make the bench leg subassemblies. Put the bench legs together to form an X, and radius the edges of the leg assembly with a router and a ¼-inch rounding-over bit. To attach the cleats to the tops of the legs, drill countersunk pilot holes, then drive 2-inch galvanized drywall-type screws through the cleats into the legs. Attach the braces to the legs, centering one end of the brace over the lap joint where the legs cross.

Radius the leg edges after the laps are cut but before the bench is assembled. Test fit two legs together, clamp them to the workbench, and run a router along the edges to be radiused. The rounded edges will flow from part to part, and you won't accidentally radius an edge that you shouldn't.

TIP

The easiest way to mount the braces on the leg subassemblies is to screw one end of the brace to a scrap of plywood, as shown. Then butt the upside-down leg subassembly against the other end of the brace. Drill pilot holes, then drive flathead wood screws through the leg's lap joint into the brace. Back out the screw that attaches the brace to the scrap plywood, and the subassembly is ready for the next step.

---

4. Lay out and cut the bench planks. Clear a space on the shop floor and lay out two of the bench planks. Use a trammel or string compass to scribe the curved edges of the benchtop. The pivot point for the outer edge should be 59¼ inches from that edge. After scribing that arc, shorten the radius of your trammel or string compass by 9¼ inches and, without moving the planks or changing the pivot point, draw the inside arc.

After drawing the arcs, mark across the ends of both boards at a 13-degree angle, as indicated in the *Bench Top View.*

Lay out the rest of the bench planks in the same manner, then cut them out with a saber saw. (Or cut out the first pair of planks and use them as templates to lay out the other planks.) Clean up the saw marks with a rasp or belt sander, then radius the edges of each plank with a router and a ¼-inch rounding-over bit.

---

5. Attach the leg assemblies to the bench planks. Position a pair of bench planks on your workbench with a ½-inch gap between them. Align the ends. Position the leg assemblies on the planks, 4 inches from each end, with the cleats running roughly parallel to the plank ends. Drill countersunk pilot holes, then drive a couple of 2-inch screws through each cleat into each plank and one through each brace into the plank.

With all three benches assembled, you are ready to complete the table.

Final assembly of the benches is straightforward. Position the bench planks, set the leg assemblies in place, drill pilot holes, then drive the screws. Your ⅜-inch electric drill can do more than bore holes; it can also drive screws into them.

TIP

Laying out the bench planks is easier than it might seem. The ideal situation is one that allows you to sketch some layout lines on the floor or a benchtop.

- Place the two planks on the work surface, about ½ inch apart, and set the trammel to the proper radius.
- Set the point on the midpoint of the outer plank's edge and scribe an arc on the work surface. The pivot point will be somewhere along this arc.
- Set the point on one corner of the inner plank and scribe an arc on the work surface. Then set the point on the opposite corner of the inner plank and scribe a second arc, intersecting the first.
- Sight (or scribe a line) from the midpoint of the outer plank to the crossing arcs. The pivot point is where this line intersects the first arc.
- Once the pivot point is located, scribe the cutting line on the outer plank, as shown in the photo. To scribe the cutting line on the inner plank, reset the trammel to the proper radius and, using the same pivot point, mark the plank.

LOCATING THE PIVOT POINT

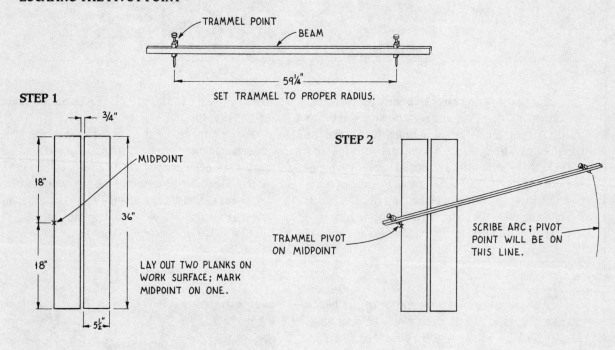

STEP 1

LAY OUT TWO PLANKS ON WORK SURFACE; MARK MIDPOINT ON ONE.

STEP 2

6. **Cut the umbrella hole in the tabletop planks and the stretcher (optional).** If you want to be able to mount a large umbrella in the table, you'll need to drill holes in the tabletop and table stretcher for the umbrella pole. Clamp the two long top planks together with a ¼-inch spacer in between. Mark the center point on the inside edge of both planks. With a hole saw of the appropriate diameter (the same as that of the pole, usually 1¾ inch), drill a hole centered between them. Depending upon the hole saw you use, you may need to bore from one side until the pilot bit emerges through the other, then flip the work over and complete the hole from the second side.

Drill a matching hole in the center of the stretcher.

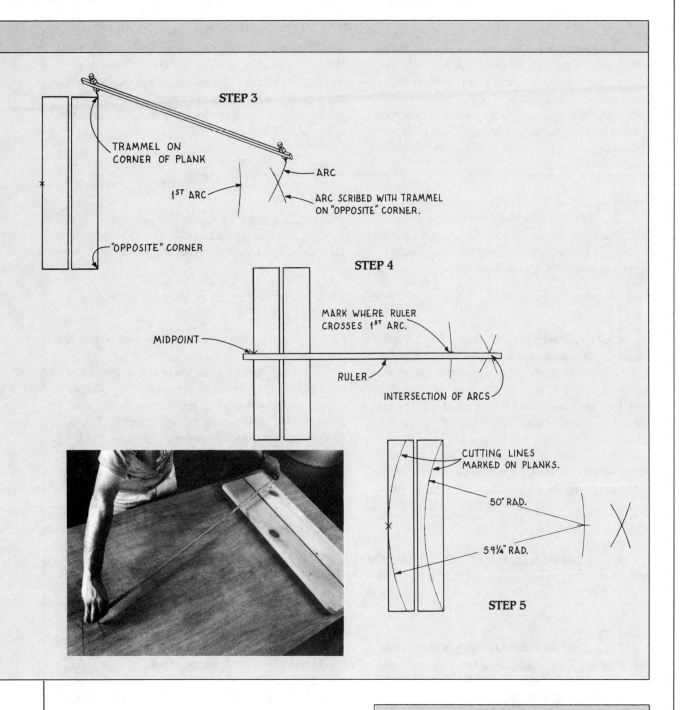

STEP 3

TRAMMEL ON
CORNER OF PLANK

ARC

ARC SCRIBED WITH TRAMMEL
ON "OPPOSITE" CORNER.

1ST ARC

"OPPOSITE" CORNER

STEP 4

MARK WHERE RULER
CROSSES 1ST ARC.

MIDPOINT

RULER

INTERSECTION OF ARCS

CUTTING LINES
MARKED ON PLANKS.

50" RAD.

59¼" RAD.

STEP 5

7. Sand the table parts. With a router and a ¼-inch rounding-over bit, radius the exposed edges of all the table parts. Dry assemble the legs to radius their edges as you did with the bench legs. Then sand all the parts of the table to remove any rough spots on the wood.

Now would be a good time to stain the parts and apply the first coat of clear finish, or, if you're painting the table, apply the first coat of paint.

TIP

If you're painting the table, apply a liberal coat of paint to parts that will be joined, and assemble them while the paint is still wet. When the paint dries, it will help seal the joints against moisture, preventing decay.

8. **Assemble the tabletop.** Measure the aprons and all the planks to find the exact middle of each, then draw a mark across the boards at this location with a pencil and try square. Set the aprons on a workbench 15⅛ inches apart. Starting at the middle of the aprons with the long top planks, tack the tabletop in place with 10d decking nails. Use scraps of ¼-inch-thick stock to space the planks evenly. Make sure you center the boards on the aprons so all the marks line up. (If the boards aren't perfectly centered on the aprons, you won't have enough stock at one end to cut a perfect circle.) When you're sure the planks are positioned correctly, drive the nails home.

9. **Saw the shape of the tabletop.** Tack a small scrap of wood over the umbrella hole in the middle of the tabletop. Drive a nail through the scrap to serve as the pivot for your string compass. Mark a circle with a radius of 22⅞ inches on the top planks.

Cut the circle with a saber saw, then clean up the saw marks with a rasp or belt sander.

10. **Assemble the table frame.** Turn the table-top over, so the aprons are up. Put the table legs together in an X, then clamp the upper ends of the legs to the aprons, positioning them as shown in the *Table Side View.* Drill ⅜-inch-diameter holes through the legs and aprons and bolt them together with ⅜-inch by 3½-inch carriage bolts, washers, and nuts.

Carefully position the stretcher so that it's centered on the lap joints of the leg-apron assemblies where the legs cross. Clamp the stretcher between the legs with a bar or pipe clamp while you install the ⅜-inch by 4-inch lag screws.

For a neat-looking installation, drill counterbores large enough to accept the lag screw washers, and deep enough so the screw heads are flush with the wood surface. Then, drill pilot holes and drive the screws through the lap joints and into the stretcher. The lag screws not only attach the legs to the stretcher, but secure the legs to each other.

11. **Install the leg braces.** With the table still upside down, set the table braces in place, as shown in the *Table Front View* and the *Table Side View.* Fasten them in position with 2½-inch screws.

12. **Add the finishing touches to the table and benches.** If necessary, use a router to round-over any remaining sharp edges. Sand all surfaces smooth, and apply the paint or finish of your choice.

We painted our table and benches, but the job wasn't as straightforward as it might seem. To extend the life of the paint, we applied a coat of a water-repellent preservative first. This we applied following the directions on the can, giving it a full 72 hours to dry. After the required time had passed, we primed the table and benches with a pigmented shellac. This both primed the surface and sealed the knots to prevent them from "bleeding" through the paint. Finally, we applied two coats of a semi-gloss latex exterior paint.

CONTOURED ENSEMBLE

Smoothly Curved for Comfort with Style

Take one look at these pieces and you can see what sets them apart from the other projects in this section. The slats are attached to curved frame members and accommodate the body a little more graciously than standard outdoor furniture. A less obvious difference is the joinery. The plans call for half-lap joints, a way of bringing two boards together that is stronger than butt joints but not very difficult to make.

CONTOURED ENSEMBLE CHAIR, BENCH, AND SWING

Although these projects may not be quite as quick and easy as the others offered in this section, their sturdy construction is worth a little extra effort.

Consider the half-lap joint that is the heart of this furniture. To make the joint, both pieces of wood give up half their thickness. The boards have a good deal of gluing surface, which helps to make a stronger union. And the steps or "shoulders" of the laps meet to further reinforce the joint.

Rodale woodworker Phil Gehret made this furni-

ture out of oak, a dense and attractive hardwood that makes its weight known the first time you pick up an assembled piece and try to move it. Lighter woods will serve well enough, among them several weather-resistant species that won't demand anything in the way of maintenance.

Laying out the curves you see here shouldn't cause you any problem, even if you can't draw a straight line. You'll read how to enlarge the scaled-down patterns using either the grid method or a pantograph. Note that

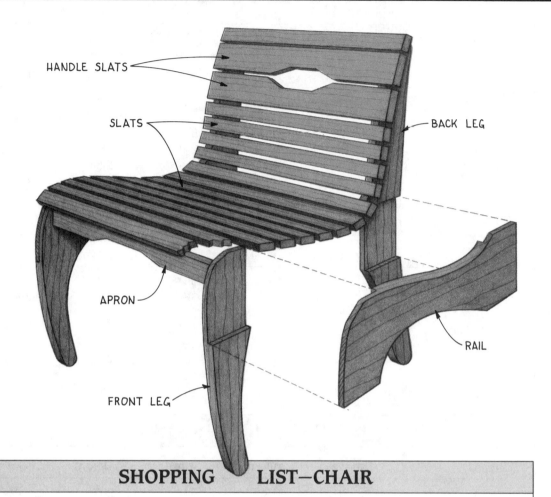

HANDLE SLATS

SLATS

BACK LEG

APRON

RAIL

FRONT LEG

SHOPPING LIST—CHAIR

LUMBER

6¼ bd. ft. 5/4 white oak
5 bd. ft. 4/4 white oak

HARDWARE AND SUPPLIES

4 pcs. #6 × 2½" galvanized drywall-type screws
32 pcs. #6 × 1¼" galvanized drywall-type screws
Resorcinol glue

FINISH

Clear water repellent or clear exterior finish

SHOPPING LIST—BENCH

LUMBER

8½ bd. ft. 5/4 white oak
10 bd. ft. 4/4 white oak

HARDWARE AND SUPPLIES

6 pcs. #6 × 2½" galvanized drywall-type screws
48 pcs. #6 × 1¼" galvanized drywall-type screws
Resorcinol glue

FINISH

Clear water repellent or clear exterior finish

SHOPPING LIST—SWING

LUMBER

7¼ bd. ft. 5/4 white oak
10 bd. ft. 4/4 white oak

HARDWARE AND SUPPLIES

4 pcs. #6 × 2½" galvanized drywall-type screws
32 pcs. #6 × 1¼" galvanized drywall-type screws
Resorcinol glue

FINISH

Clear water repellent or clear exterior finish

CUTTING LIST—CHAIR

PIECE	NUMBER	THICKNESS	WIDTH	LENGTH	MATERIAL
Back legs	2	1⅟₁₆"	5½"	29"	5/4 oak
Front legs	2	1⅟₁₆"	3½"	15"	5/4 oak
Rails	2	1⅟₁₆"	5½"	23"	5/4 oak
Apron	1	¾"	2¼"	17⅞"	4/4 oak
Handle slats	2	¾"	2¼"	22"	4/4 oak
Slats	14	¾"	1½"	22"	4/4 oak

CUTTING LIST—BENCH

PIECE	NUMBER	THICKNESS	WIDTH	LENGTH	MATERIAL
Back legs	2	1⅟₁₆"	5½"	29"	5/4 oak
Front legs	2	1⅟₁₆"	3½"	15"	5/4 oak
Rails	2	1⅟₁₆"	5½"	23"	5/4 oak
Center back	1	1⅟₁₆"	5½"	20"	5/4 oak
Center rail	1	1⅟₁₆"	5½"	21"	5/4 oak
Apron	1	¾"	2¼"	41⅞"	4/4 oak
Handle slats	2	¾"	2¼"	46"	4/4 oak
Slats	14	¾"	1½"	46"	4/4 oak

CUTTING LIST—SWING

PIECE	NUMBER	THICKNESS	WIDTH	LENGTH	MATERIAL
Backs	3	1⅟₁₆"	5½"	20"	5/4 oak
Rails	2	1⅟₁₆"	5½"	23"	5/4 oak
Center rail	1	1⅟₁₆"	5½"	21"	5/4 oak
Apron	1	¾"	2¼"	41⅞"	4/4 oak
Handle slats	2	¾"	2¼"	46"	4/4 oak
Slats	14	¾"	1½"	46"	4/4 oak

all or part of the curved frame pattern is used in each piece of the ensemble. The full frame occurs in the chair and bench; it loses its legs for the swing and the middle frame of the bench. In the following project, a table borrows only the front leg and its mirror image. Note that in both the bench and swing, the middle frame is cut short at the front edge to accommodate the apron.

Builder's Notes

The lap joint used in this project is a step up from the butt joint, but it remains a simpler affair than a mortise-and-tenon or dovetail joint. Although you can use a router, circular saw, or table saw to cut the laps, the work will go faster with a radial arm saw equipped with a dado cutter.

Materials. The furniture shown is made of oak. The decay resistance of oak depends on the particular species; white oak is one of the better woods in this respect, while red oak is among the less resistant. Unless protected with a clear finish, oak will be darkened by precipitation. Woods that weather without such dramatic discoloration include redwood, cedar, mahogany, and cypress. Pine is both affordable and readily available, but it needs to be varnished or painted to extend its useful life.

As is the case with all hardwoods, oak is not a dimension lumber, which means it isn't stocked at every lumberyard and it isn't available in predictable sizes.

PATTERNS

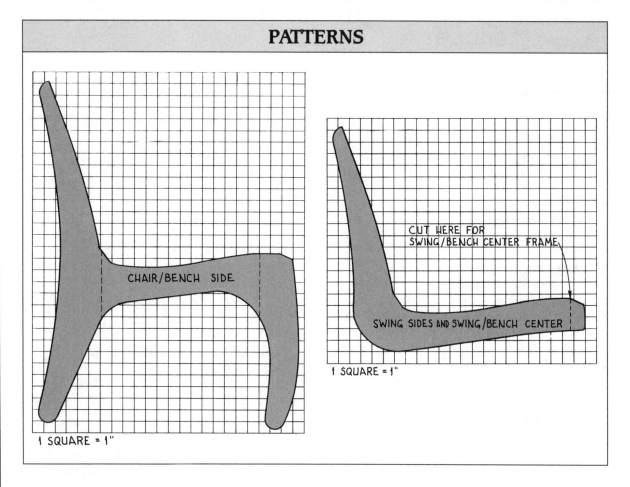

CHAIR/BENCH SIDE

1 SQUARE = 1"

CUT HERE FOR
SWING/BENCH CENTER FRAME

SWING SIDES AND SWING/BENCH CENTER

1 SQUARE = 1"

Thicknesses are standardized, but not widths and lengths.

The thicknesses are couched in terms of quarters of an inch. A four-quarter (4/4) board is actually ¾ inch thick; the missing ¼ inch is lost to the shrinkage that accompanies drying and to the planing that smooths the board. Similarly, a 5/4 (five-quarter) board is 1 1/16 inches thick, an 8/4 board 1¾ inches thick.

The "Shopping List" for the bench specifies the purchase of 8½ board feet of 5/4 oak. With hardwoods, you must keep the dimensions of the necessary parts in mind when you shop. A board might contain the requisite number of board feet without having the correct dimensions to give you the parts you need. Remember that you may have to work around knots and other defects, so be prepared to buy more wood than you strictly need.

Although the plans call for the frames to be made out of 5/4 stock, you can adapt these projects to use standard 2 × 4s and 2 × 6s.

Tools and techniques. The core procedure in building these pieces is making rectilinear frames. The horizontal member is joined to the two verticals with lap joints. The laps are best cut with a dado blade on a radial arm saw. You can do the job with a dado blade on a table saw, but you won't be able to see the blade in the act of cutting. A circular saw or router will also handle half-laps.

The joints are glued together; screws aren't necessary. Finally, the full-size pattern is traced on these rough frames and then cut out with a saber saw.

As with other projects in this book, these pieces will come together more quickly if you use an electric drill or drill-driver to sink the drywall-type screws. Driving more than a few screws by hand gets to be a chore. If you will be using drywall screws in oak, plan on drilling pilot holes; this step is a help but not a requirement with softer woods.

Finish. Three prime considerations in choosing an exterior wood finish (in no particular order) are: what the finish looks like, the conditions under which the wood will be used, and the kind of wood you are finishing.

The last consideration may be the first you look at. If you, like us, build your contoured furniture pieces of oak (or another hardwood), you will undoubtedly avoid any finish that will obscure the wood's figure and color. You'll use a clear (or natural) finish such as an exterior-

TOOL LIST

Belt sander	Router
Circular saw	¼" rounding-over bit
Clamps	Ruler
Drill	Saber saw
Pilot hole bit	Sandpaper
Finishing sander	Sawhorses
Paintbrush	Screwdriver
Plug cutter	Tack cloth
Radial arm saw	Tape measure
Dado set	Try square

Like every other outdoor finish, you must renew penetrating oil every couple of years.

Neither of these finishes does the best job of protecting wood outdoors. That job is done by paint. If you build of pine, you ought to give prime consideration to paint. Paint has more pigment than other finishes, and pigment is what blocks out the sun's degrading effects. Also, paint forms a film on the wood (instead of soaking in, as stain does), which further retards erosion. In general, oil-based paints are more resistant to moisture than latex paints.

grade varnish or an exterior-grade penetrating oil.

Varnishes, including urethane, provide a beautiful natural finish, but unfortunately, they don't hold up outdoors unless protected from direct exposure to sunlight. Varnish forms a film, which can peel. To develop the most durable film, varnish manufacturers recommend applying three to six thin coats.

Penetrating oil, in contrast, is easy to apply. You brush on a generous application and let it penetrate the wood. Before it has time to completely dry, you apply a second coat. Then you are done. It takes the oil 48 to 72 hours to completely dry and for the odor to disappear.

TOP VIEW

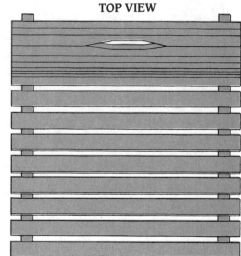

CHAIR PLAN VIEWS

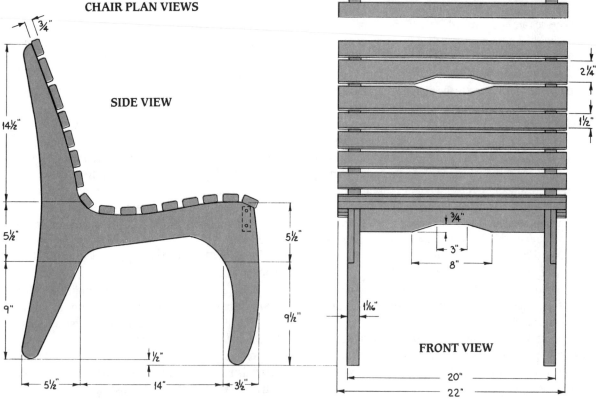

SIDE VIEW

FRONT VIEW

BENCH PLAN VIEWS

TOP VIEW

FRONT VIEW

SIDE VIEW

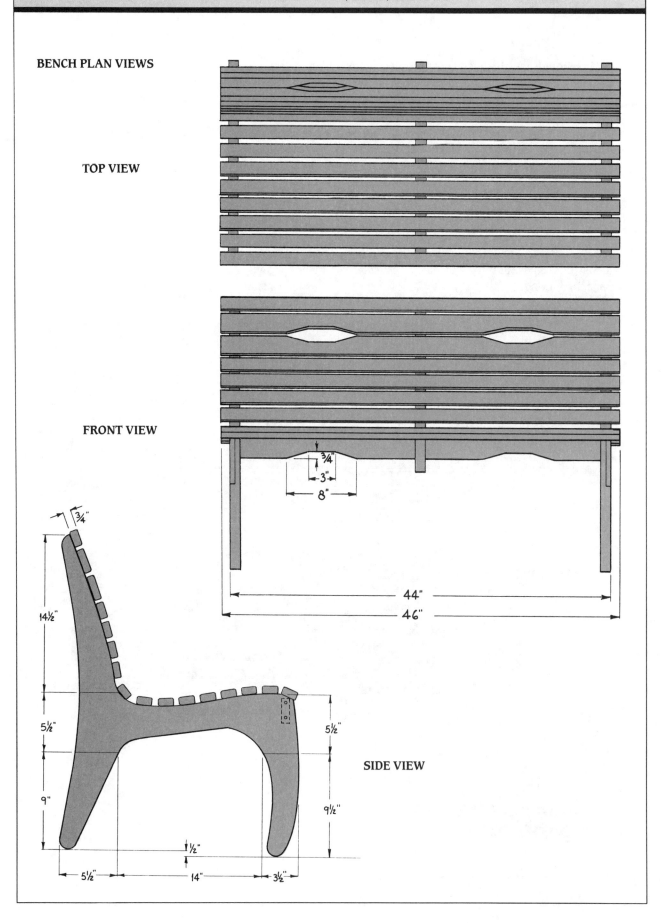

1. **Rough-cut the back legs, front legs, and rails.** The basic frames are the side and center rails. (The chairs require only side rails; the bench and the swing are wide enough that the slats need extra support in the middle, which the center rail provides.) Although these rails have a curved contour in the finished furniture pieces, they are assembled of rectilinear boards.

The side frames for the chair and bench are identical,

each being formed of a front and a back leg connected by a rail. The swing's side frames obviously don't have legs, and neither do the center frames required for the bench and swing.

Begin making the seating project you have chosen by cutting the legs and rails to the lengths specified by the "Cutting List."

2. **Cut the lap joints.** Lay out the half-lap joints on the boards, as shown in the *Rough Frame Assemblies* drawing.

Although you can use any number of tools to cut laps—beginning with a backsaw and ranging through router, circular saw, and table saw—we found the *best*

SWING PLAN VIEWS

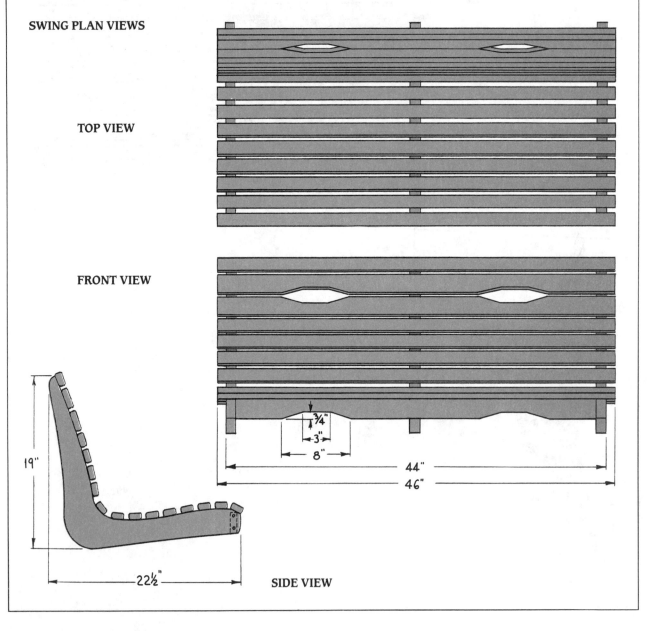

TOP VIEW

FRONT VIEW

SIDE VIEW

tool to cut these particular laps was the radial arm saw.

To make fast work of this operation, fit the saw with a dada cutter to remove as much waste as possible with each pass, and clamp a stop block to the saw fence to accurately control the length of each lap. Adjust the blade height to cut halfway through the 5/4 stock. Although the depth of the cut is crucial, the exact placement of the laps is not. That's because you will be cutting out the curved frame from this rough assembly. If one board sticks a bit beyond another, the error will be cut away and consigned to the scrap pile.

Work methodically to avoid getting the joints mixed up. All are cut to the same depth, but there are two different lengths, and the laps on the back legs are T-laps rather than end laps. So set your stop block for the front legs first, and cut the laps on those. Use the same setting to lap the back ends of the rails. Reset the stop block and lap the front ends of the rails. Finally, set two stop blocks to lap the back legs.

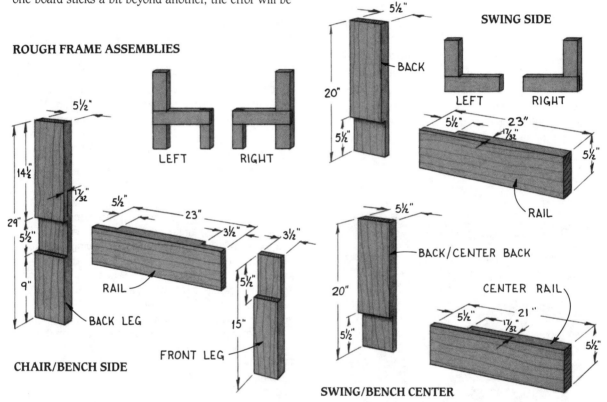

ROUGH FRAME ASSEMBLIES

CHAIR/BENCH SIDE

SWING SIDE

SWING/BENCH CENTER

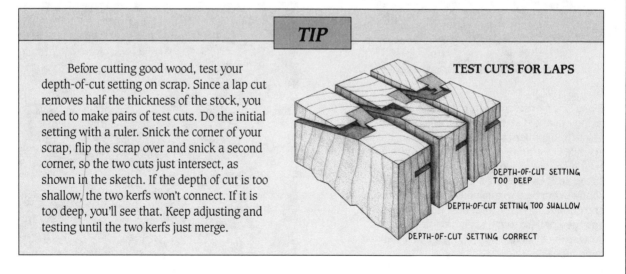

TIP

Before cutting good wood, test your depth-of-cut setting on scrap. Since a lap cut removes half the thickness of the stock, you need to make pairs of test cuts. Do the initial setting with a ruler. Snick the corner of your scrap, flip the scrap over and snick a second corner, so the two cuts just intersect, as shown in the sketch. If the depth of cut is too shallow, the two kerfs won't connect. If it is too deep, you'll see that. Keep adjusting and testing until the two kerfs just merge.

TEST CUTS FOR LAPS

DEPTH-OF-CUT SETTING TOO DEEP

DEPTH-OF-CUT SETTING TOO SHALLOW

DEPTH-OF-CUT SETTING CORRECT

3. Glue up the frames. Once you're certain that the surfaces of the lap joints are smooth and consistent, assemble the frames using resorcinol glue.

Note that you have to make a left side frame and a right side frame; the two are not identical, they are mirror images. Ideally, when you look at the assembled chair (or bench or swing), the horizontal line of the rail is unbroken. To avoid mix-ups, assemble the left and right frames side by side, as shown in the *Rough Frame Assemblies* drawing.

4. Enlarge the frame pattern and transfer it to the rough frames. Enlarge the patterns as accurately as possible. An indifferent job of laying out these curved lines can spoil the project.

The grid method of enlarging a pattern is simple and traditional. Note the grid superimposed on the frame patterns. To make a full-size pattern, lay out a 1-inch grid on a sheet of paper measuring at least 23 by 29 inches for the chair or bench, and at least 19 by 23 inches for the swing. (If you are making only the swing, you needn't bother drawing the legs.) Next, transfer reference points from the grid in the book to the one you've drawn: These are the points at which the outline of the frame pattern crosses a grid line. Finally, play "connect the dots" with the points you've plotted on the large grid. Don't just draw lines; try to fair them into graceful curves that come close to those in the book's pattern.

If you don't trust yourself with even this level of freehand drawing, you can use a pantograph, a drafting device that consists of two inverted, interlocking Vs. As you trace the original drawing with a stylus, a pencil point on another arm of the pantograph draws a larger (or smaller) version with good accuracy. Pantographs are available at art supply and drafting stores.

Right: You can enlarge any pattern in this book by laying out a grid at the scale specified, then plotting points from pattern to grid. If, for example, the pattern specifies "1 square = 1"," you must draw a grid with 1-inch squares. (You don't, however, have to grid the "dead spaces" on the pattern; only grid the general shape of the pattern outline.) After plotting the points and connecting them freehand, go back over the enlarged pattern with a straightedge and French curves or a flexible curve, giving it a well-defined, continuous contour.

Left: A pantograph looks ungainly, and, frankly, it is. But it can help you make pattern enlargements fairly quickly. The device is mounted on a drawing board or on a piece of smooth plywood and adjusted to the scale of enlargement necessary. With the stylus, trace around the pattern in the book, and the pantograph's pencil will produce a rough enlargement. "Rough" means the lines will waver and wander; you will need to use a straightedge and flexible curve to align the straights and contour the curves, as shown here. Though it seems double work, it still is faster than drawing a grid and plotting points.

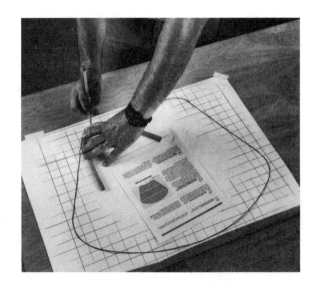

There are a couple of ways to transfer the outline of the frame from the full-size pattern to the rough frame assemblies. You can place sheets of carbon paper between the pattern and the wood, then tape the pattern in place and trace along the outline. Or, turn the pattern over and draw a wide, heavy line where you see the outline through the paper, using a soft (number one) pencil. Then flip the pattern right-side up, tape it in place, and use a harder pencil to trace with enough pressure to leave a line of graphite on the wood.

If you plan on making a number of pieces—the complete ensemble, perhaps, or a few chairs—you may want to make a durable template. This cut-out pattern is used to trace the outline on frames.

If you are making the bench or swing, note that the pattern shows that the front edge of the center frame must be cut short in order to accommodate the apron that will run across the piece.

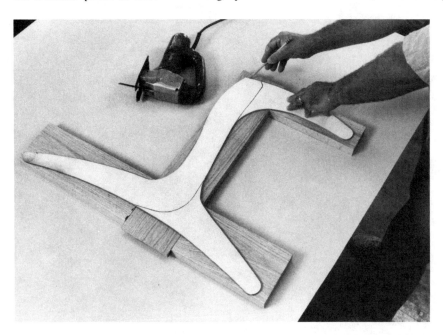

To make a template, enlarge the pattern onto something more durable than a sheet of paper (we used lauan plywood) and cut it out. You also can use cardboard, posterboard, or Masonite (hardboard). Place the template on each side assembly and trace around it. Note that the template shown is marked with lines that show where to eliminate the legs for the swing frames and the middle bench frame; you can use the entire template for chair and bench end frames, then saw off the template's legs and use it to lay out these smaller frames.

5. **Cut out the frames.** Use a saber saw to cut out the frames, taking care not to stray inside the line. If necessary, use a belt sander, hand plane, or file to remove excess wood down to the line. Use a router and a ¼-inch rounding-over bit to radius all edges.

Even though this frame is made of 5/4 oak, a saber saw can manage the job. Clamp the workpiece to a bench or sawhorse, making sure that the area to be sawed is cantilevered out over the edge of the support.

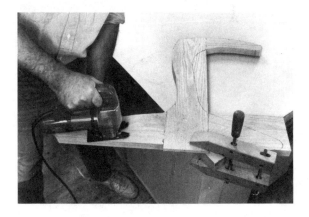

6. **Cut the apron and slats.** Cut the apron, 14 narrow (1½ inch) slats, and two wide (2¼ inch) handle slats. Lay out the cutouts in one edge of the apron and in both handle slats, as shown in the *Plan Views.* Make the cutouts with a saber saw. Again, use a router and a ¼-inch rounding-over bit to radius all edges.

7. Assemble the chair. With a helper, attach the slats and apron to the frames. Use screws, driven into counterbored pilot holes, then cover the screws with wood plugs glued into the counterbores. Sink one 1¼-inch screw in either end of each slat, and two 2½-inch screws through either side of the frame and into the apron. On the bench and swing, drive two additional 2½-inch screws through the apron and into the front edge of the center frame.

Make the plugs from scraps of the working stock, using a plug cutter. Apply resorcinol glue to the counterbores with a cotton swab. To make the plugs as inconspicuous as possible, try to pick plugs that match the wood's color, and align the plug's grain with the surrounding grain.

8. Apply a finish. Sand the piece with fine-grit sandpaper. If the wood needs to be protected from the elements, apply a clear finish or exterior paint.

CONTOURED ENSEMBLE TABLE

An ensemble is a group working together to achieve a single effect. In outdoor furniture terms, you have an ensemble when the different furniture pieces have the same aesthetic appearance. Though the pieces function differently, they work together visually.

This table, though it serves a different function from the contoured chair and bench, clearly springs from the same aesthetic. If you've built the contoured bench or chair, or the lounger that follows, and you want to add a table, then you'll surely choose a complementary design. And this table not only uses the same materials and joinery, it borrows part of the chair's side pattern for its legs. (If a contoured chair were to mutate into an end table, this is what you'd get.)

The construction process is a virtual repeat of the chair's: Make up the leg frames using lap joints, cut the curvilinear shape, and screw the slats and aprons to the leg assemblies to complete the construction.

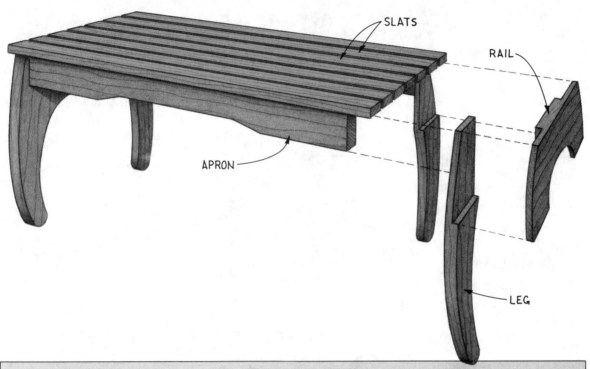

SHOPPING LIST

LUMBER
3½ bd. ft. 5/4 white oak
4 bd. ft. 4/4 white oak

HARDWARE AND SUPPLIES
8 pcs. #6 × 2½" galvanized drywall-type screws
14 pcs. #6 × 1¼" galvanized drywall-type screws
Resorcinol glue

FINISH
Clear water repellent or clear exterior finish

CUTTING LIST

PIECE	NUMBER	THICKNESS	WIDTH	LENGTH	MATERIAL
Legs	4	1¹⁄₁₆"	3½"	15"	5/4 oak
Rails	2	1¹⁄₁₆"	5½"	15"	5/4 oak
Aprons	3	¾"	2¼"	27⅞"	4/4 oak
Slats	7	¾"	1½"	32"	4/4 oak

Builder's Notes

The construction of the contoured table closely mimics that of the chair (or bench or swing). If you are building only the table, by all means read over the "Builder's Notes" for the chair on page 56 before you begin cutting wood. In addition, skim through the step-by-step section as well; it details the best way to cut the laps and assemble the side frames, how to enlarge the patterns, and so forth. The building tips there may prove useful in constructing the table.

PATTERN

1 SQUARE = 1"

TOOL LIST

Belt sander	Router
Drill	¼" rounding-over bit
Countersink bit	Ruler
Pilot hole bit	Saber saw
Plug cutter	Sandpaper
Finishing sander	Sawhorses
Hand screws	Screwdriver
Paintbrush	Tack cloth
Radial arm saw	Tape measure
Dado set	Try square

PLAN VIEWS

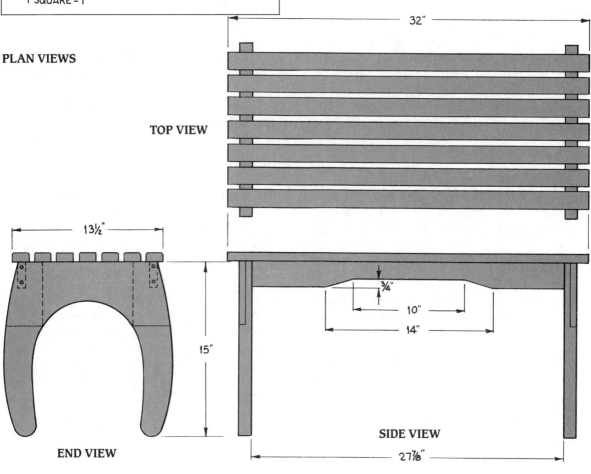

TOP VIEW

32"

13½"

15"

¾"

10"

14"

END VIEW

SIDE VIEW

27⅞"

1. **Cut the legs and rails.** Cut the parts needed to make a pair of rough frames to the sizes specified by the "Cutting List." Each frame consists of two legs bridged at the top by a rail.

2. **Cut the laps and glue up the frames.** Lay out the laps on the legs and rails. Cut them on a radial arm saw equipped with a dado cutter.

Once you're certain that the surfaces of the lap joints are smooth and consistent, assemble the frames using resorcinol glue. Clamp the assemblies with hand screws. Note that both frames are identical.

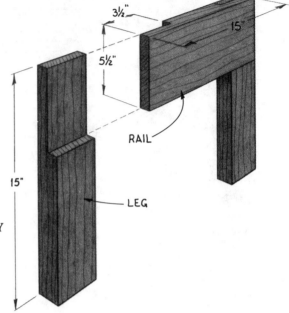

ROUGH END FRAME ASSEMBLY

3. **Cut the frames to their final contour.** Enlarge the frame pattern and transfer it to the rough frames. The table derives its charm from the legs, so take care when laying them out.

For cutting the contours, use a saber saw. If you stray from the line, it should be to the outside of the pattern, into waste wood. Use a belt sander to remove any excess wood down to that line.

Using a router and a ¼-inch rounding-over bit, radius all but the top edges.

4. **Cut the aprons and slats.** Note the cutouts in the aprons; lay them out, as shown in the *Side View,* and cut them with a saber saw or band saw. Again, use a router and a ¼-inch rounding-over bit to radius all edges of the slats and the lower edges of the aprons.

5. **Assemble the table.** Attach the slats and aprons to the frames. Note that the frames are juxtaposed so that, when the assembled table is viewed from each end, the rails will be seen to overlap the legs. To assemble the parts, use screws, driving them into counterbored pilot holes. Cover the screws with wood plugs glued into the counterbores. Sink one 1¼-inch screw through each end of each slat, and two 2½-inch screws through each frame and into the aprons.

Make the plugs from scraps of the working stock, using a plug cutter. Apply resorcinol glue to the counterbores with a cotton swab. To make the plugs as inconspicuous as possible, try to pick plugs that match the wood's color, and align the plug's grain with the surrounding grain.

6. **Apply a finish.** Sand the table with fine-grit sandpaper. If you've chosen a wood that needs to be protected from the weather, apply a clear finish or exterior paint.

CONTOURED ENSEMBLE CHAISE LOUNGE

Here is a rakish chaise lounge to complete the Contoured Ensemble. The back is fixed, sparing you the trouble of dealing with any hardware. The lines are graceful, and seem to advertise that this is a comfortable place to relax.

This project has something in common with its ensemble kin. Take a look at the front legs, and you'll see that they are the same as those on the chair, bench, and table. The back legs, though different from the others in the set, are true to the ensemble's style. The side rails and backs add their own sinuous curves.

Structurally, the two side frames, which look like elongated versions of those on the other furniture, are the core. The rails meet the legs in half-lap joints, forming the side frames. The slats tie the two frames together.

SHOPPING LIST

LUMBER

10¼ bd. ft. 5/4 white oak
9¼ bd. ft. 4/4 white oak

HARDWARE AND SUPPLIES

8 pcs. #6 × 2½" galvanized drywall-type screws
62 pcs. #6 × 1¼" galvanized drywall-type screws
Resorcinol glue

FINISH

Clear water repellent or clear exterior finish

CUTTING LIST

PIECE	NUMBER	THICKNESS	WIDTH	LENGTH	MATERIAL
Front legs	2	1¹⁄₁₆"	3½"	15"	5/4 × 4 oak
Back legs	2	1¹⁄₁₆"	3½"	16"	5/4 × 4 oak
Rails	2	1¹⁄₁₆"	5½"	60"	5/4 × 6 oak
Backs	2	1¹⁄₁₆"	3½"	28"	5/4 × 4 oak
Apron	1	¾"	2¼"	19⅞"	5/4 × 3 oak
Brace	1	¾"	3"	19⅞"	4/4 × 4 oak
Handle slats	2	¾"	2¼"	24"	4/4 × 3 oak
Slats	29	¾"	1½"	24"	4/4 × 2 oak

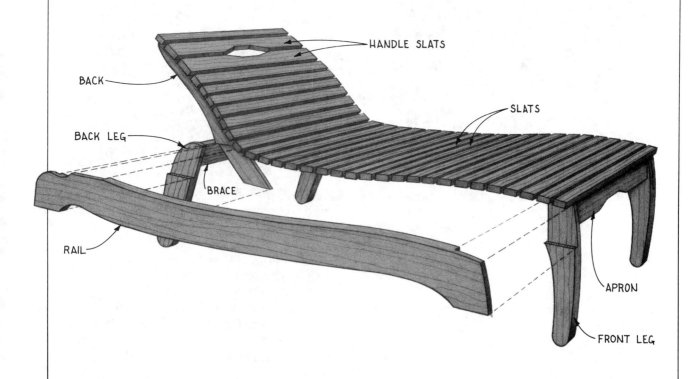

PLAN VIEWS

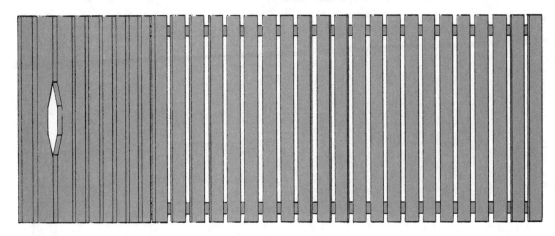

TOP VIEW

SIDE VIEW

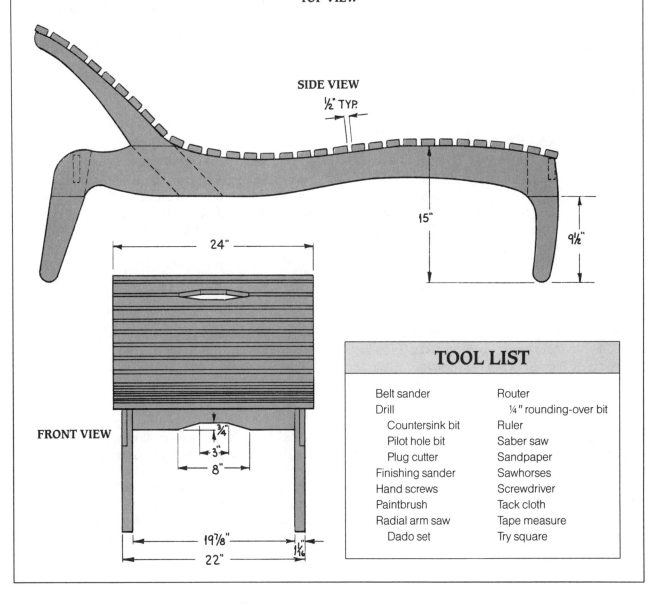

½" TYP.

15"

9½"

24"

FRONT VIEW

¾"
3"
8"

19⅞"
1¼"
22"

TOOL LIST

Belt sander	Router
Drill	¼" rounding-over bit
Countersink bit	Ruler
Pilot hole bit	Saber saw
Plug cutter	Sandpaper
Finishing sander	Sawhorses
Hand screws	Screwdriver
Paintbrush	Tack cloth
Radial arm saw	Tape measure
Dado set	Try square

PATTERN

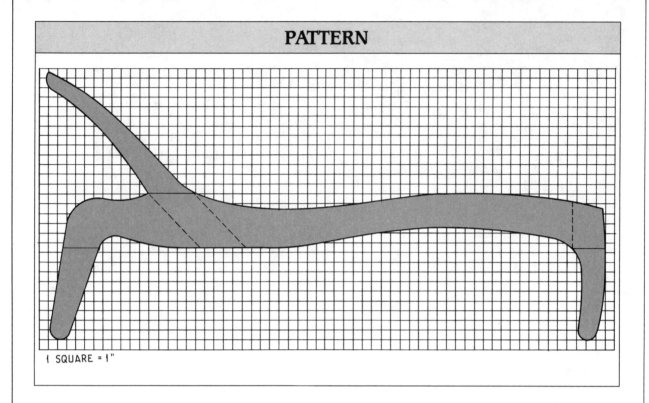

1 SQUARE = 1"

Builder's Notes

The construction of the contoured chaise lounge closely mimics that of the chair (or bench or swing). If you are building only the lounger, by all means read over the "Builder's Notes" for the chair on page 56 before you begin cutting wood. In addition, skim through the step-by-step section as well; it details the best way to cut the laps and assemble the side frames, how to enlarge the patterns, and so forth. The building tips there may prove useful in constructing this project.

1. Cut the legs, rails, and backs. Cut the parts of the two frames, each consisting of two legs, a back, and a rail. The chaise has an additional pair of half-laps, where the backs meet the rails. Otherwise, the procedure for making the two frames is similar to that given for the other projects this chapter.

2. Make the lap joints. Lay out the lap joints on the boards, making sure that you will be able to cut out the finished shapes of the legs and backs at the correct angles. The back leg is canted 10 degrees from the rail, and the back is canted 45 degrees. The front leg is at a standard 90 degree angle. Note also that you have to make a left frame and a right frame; the two are not identical. The laps will be cut in the *insides* of the rails.

So, when you look at the assembled lounge from either side, the legs and the back will be seen to pass behind the rail. We found that the best tool for cutting the laps is a radial arm saw equipped with a dado blade, though you could use a router or circular saw.

Check that the surfaces of the lap joints are smooth and consistent. Then glue up the frames using resorcinol glue.

ROUGH SIDE FRAME ASSEMBLY

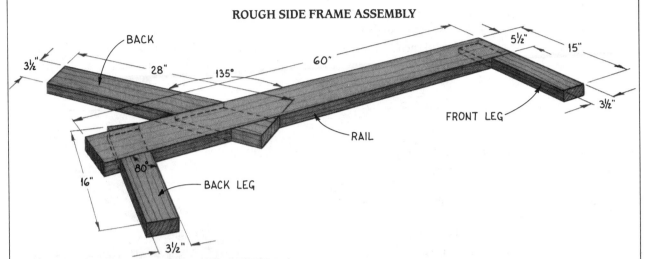

Left: Cutting the half-laps with the radial arm saw, a good tool to use for this task. Since you move the cutter over the workpiece, you can see the cut you are making as you make it. Also, the workpiece is stationary while the cut is being made. Since the chaise sides are large (and heavy, if you are using oak), this is a distinct safety advantage. After each pass, you shift the position of the workpiece.

Below: Gluing up a rough frame for the chaise. Mix resorcinol glue in a paper cup, and use a cheap brush to apply it. The hand screws shown distribute their clamping pressure over a broad area, but you can also use bar clamps or C-clamps.

3. Cut the frame contours. Draw a full-size copy of the pattern given here. Make sure your drawing captures the grace of the plan's curves. Then transfer the full-size pattern onto the rough frames.

Use a saber saw to cut out the frames; they will be too unwieldy to cut on the band saw. Take care not to stray inside the line. If necessary, use a belt sander to remove excess wood down to the line. Finally, use a router with a ¼-inch rounding-over bit to radius all the edges that will be exposed on the completed project.

4. Cut the apron, brace, and slats. Cut the apron, brace, narrow (1½ inch) slats, and the wide (2¼ inch) handle slats, as specified by the "Cutting List." Lay out the cutouts in one edge of the apron and the handle slats, and in both edges of the brace, as shown in the *Typical Cutout* drawing. Make the cutouts with a saber saw. Again, use a router with a ¼-inch rounding-over bit to radius the exposed edges of each slat and the apron.

TYPICAL CUTOUT

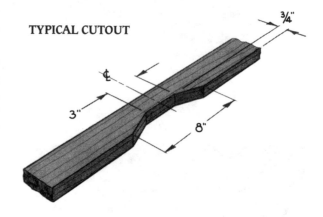

5. Assemble the chaise. With a helper, attach the slats, apron, and brace to the frames. Use screws, driven into counterbored pilot holes, then cover the screws with wood plugs glued into the counterbores. Sink one 1¼-inch screw in each end of every slat. Use two 2½-inch screws through either side of the frame and into the apron and brace.

Make the plugs from scraps of the working stock, using a plug cutter. Apply resorcinol glue to the counterbores with a cotton swab. To make the plugs as inconspicuous as possible, try to pick plugs that match the wood's color, and align the plug's grain with the surrounding grain.

Cutting plugs is done with a plug cutter, which can be chucked in a drill press or a hand-held power drill. To get loose plugs—like dowels—simply bore completely through the stock; each new plug you cut will eject the previous one from the cutter. But you can also stop the boring and leave the plugs attached to the stock. When you need one, break it out with a screwdriver or chisel.

6. Apply a finish. Go over the chaise with fine-grit sandpaper. If the wood needs to be protected from the elements, apply a clear finish or exterior paint.

ADIRONDACK ENSEMBLE

Inexpensive Lawn Classics

This chair with ottoman, matching settee, and side table is at home on the lawn, porch, or deck, be it at your Adirondack camp or just out in the backyard.

ADIRONDACK ENSEMBLE CHAIR WITH OTTOMAN

The Adirondack chair has become one of the classic pieces of outdoor furniture. Its flat-board, angular design is right at home in the backyard or on the deck or porch. Typically, it's parked on the lawn and left there all summer.

This popular chair apparently evolved from one called the Westport, which was designed and patented around the turn of the century. It was named for a small town in New York's Adirondack region. The Westport has the same simple, angular planes, but the back and seat are not slatted.

The chair is the mainstay of our ensemble, and you'll probably want to make several of them. The matching ottoman transforms the chair into a chaise lounge, which allows you to stick your feet up so you'll be sittin' easy.

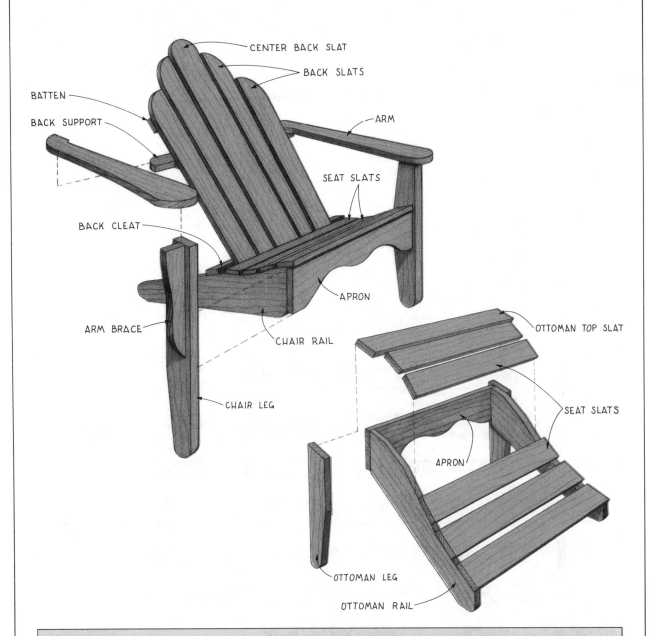

CENTER BACK SLAT

BACK SLATS

BATTEN

BACK SUPPORT

ARM

SEAT SLATS

BACK CLEAT

ARM BRACE

APRON

CHAIR RAIL

CHAIR LEG

OTTOMAN TOP SLAT

SEAT SLATS

APRON

OTTOMAN LEG

OTTOMAN RAIL

SHOPPING LIST

LUMBER

1 pc. 5/4 × 6 × 12′ #2 white pine
1 pc. 5/4 × 4 × 10′ #2 white pine
1 pc. 1 × 6 × 12′ #2 white pine*
2 pcs. 1 × 4 × 10′ #2 white pine
1 pc. 1 × 4 × 8′ #2 white pine
1 pc. 1 × 3 × 4′ #2 white pine

HARDWARE AND SUPPLIES

1 box #6 × 1¼″ galvanized drywall-type screws
1 box #6 × 1⅝″ galvanized drywall-type screws

HARDWARE AND SUPPLIES—CONTINUED

1 box #6 × 2″ galvanized drywall-type screws
Wood putty
Resorcinol glue

FINISH

Exterior paint or clear finish of your choice

*Try to get one with two clear 30″ lengths from which to cut the arms.

CUTTING LIST

PIECE	NUMBER	THICKNESS	WIDTH	LENGTH	MATERIAL
Chair rails	2	1¹⁄₁₆"	5½"	31½"	5/4 × 6 pine
Chair legs	2	1¹⁄₁₆"	3½"	21½"	5/4 × 4 pine
Ottoman rails	2	1¹⁄₁₆"	5½"	24"	5/4 × 6 pine
Ottoman legs	2	1¹⁄₁₆"	3½"	15½"	5/4 × 6 pine
Aprons	2	¾"	5½"	21½"	1 × 6 pine
Back cleat	1	1¹⁄₁₆"	3½"	21½"	5/4 × 4 pine
Back support	1	1¹⁄₁₆"	3½"	28½"	5/4 × 4 pine
Arms	2	¾"	5½"	29"	1 × 6 pine*
Center back slat	1	¾"	5½"	35½"	1 × 6 pine
Long back slats	2	¾"	3½"	33"	1 × 4 pine
Short back slats	2	¾"	3½"	29½"	1 × 4 pine
Arm braces	2	1¹⁄₁₆"	3"	10"	5/4 × 4 pine
Batten	1	¾"	2½"	20"	1 × 3 pine
Seat slats	9	¾"	3½"	21½"	1 × 4 pine
Ottoman top slat	1	¾"	2½"	23⅝"	1 × 3 pine

*Cut from knot-clear piece of #2 pine.

CUTTING DIAGRAM

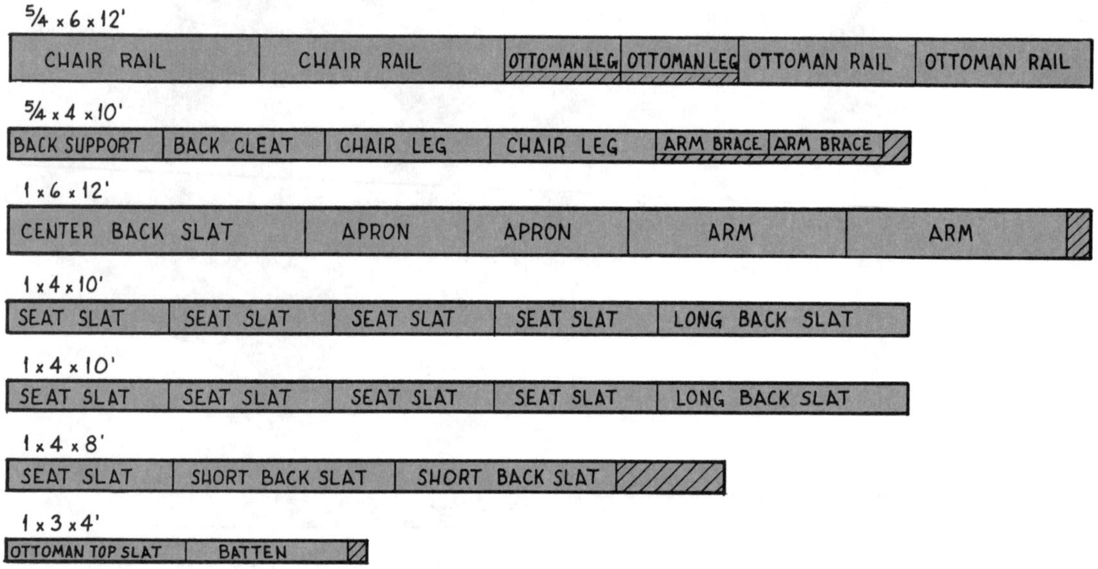

⁵⁄₄ × 6 × 12'
| CHAIR RAIL | CHAIR RAIL | OTTOMAN LEG | OTTOMAN LEG | OTTOMAN RAIL | OTTOMAN RAIL |

⁵⁄₄ × 4 × 10'
| BACK SUPPORT | BACK CLEAT | CHAIR LEG | CHAIR LEG | ARM BRACE | ARM BRACE |

1 × 6 × 12'
| CENTER BACK SLAT | APRON | APRON | ARM | ARM |

1 × 4 × 10'
| SEAT SLAT | SEAT SLAT | SEAT SLAT | SEAT SLAT | LONG BACK SLAT |

1 × 4 × 10'
| SEAT SLAT | SEAT SLAT | SEAT SLAT | SEAT SLAT | LONG BACK SLAT |

1 × 4 × 8'
| SEAT SLAT | SHORT BACK SLAT | SHORT BACK SLAT |

1 × 3 × 4'
| OTTOMAN TOP SLAT | BATTEN |

Comfortable chairs are usually considered difficult to construct. This one is not. The look of the chair belies its comfort. It *is* comfortable. And its construction *is* simple.

Because we planned to paint the set—white is common, but bright primary colors are great!—we used pine. Use waterproof glue, galvanized fasteners, and freshen the paint every couple of years, and your Adirondack ensemble will last for decades.

Builder's Notes

This set is easy to build. Many of the components are laid out from patterns, then cut out with a saber saw or band saw. The hardest job may well be that of enlarging all the patterns.

Materials. As with most outdoor furniture projects, you have several choices in woods, depending on what's readily available in your area. You can use a hard-

PATTERNS

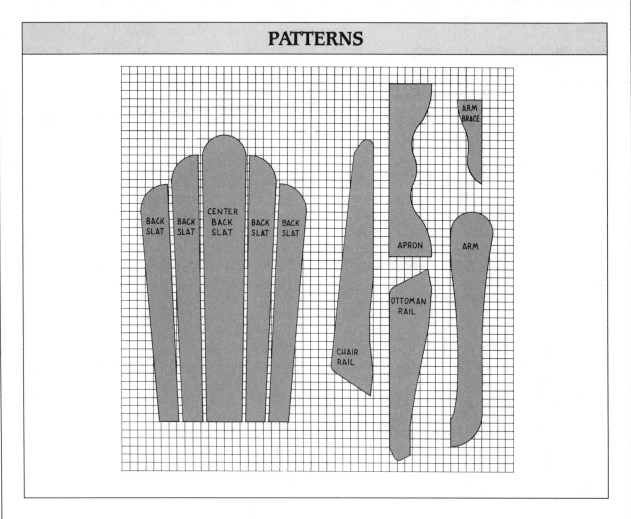

wood, such as oak or birch, covered with a clear exterior finish such as marine-grade spar varnish or exterior polyurethane. Redwood or red cedar are good choices when it comes to natural decay resistance and weatherability; pressure-treated wood is even more durable.

Because we planned to paint the set, we used #2 white pine. All of the pieces in the ensemble are cut from 1-by dimensional lumber (¾-inch dressed thickness) and 5/4 (five-quarter) stock (1¹⁄₁₆-inch dressed thickness).

For assembly, use resorcinol glue, which is waterproof, and galvanized drywall-type screws, which are tailor-made for use with power screwdrivers.

Tools and techniques. This ensemble is very much a band saw project. We used one to round the ends of the legs and slats, taper the legs, and cut out the shaped parts shown in the patterns. If you don't have access to a band saw, a saber saw will do; the lumber thicknesses are within its capacity. Use a router and a ¼-inch rounding-over bit to radius the exposed edges of the various components.

Although most of the cuts are simple, making

clean, accurate taper cuts for the legs and back slats will require a bit of skill. After laying out the pattern on the stock, we used the band saw to cut the tapered sides just outside the marked line, then planed down to the line with a block plane.

With all the screws used to assemble the furniture

TOOL LIST

Band saw	Saber saw
Block plane	Sander(s)
Clamps	Sandpaper
Drill	Saw for crosscutting
Countersink bit	Saw for ripping
Pilot hole bit	Sawhorses
Framing square	Screwdriver
Paintbrush	Tack cloth
Router	Tape measure
¼ " rounding-over bit	Try square

in this ensemble, you need a good pilot hole bit, which consists of a tapered bit, a countersink, and a stop collar. The girth of the bit is matched to the screw gauge, and you adjust the bit to alter the depth of the pilot hole.

Patterns. Enlarge the patterns reproduced here to make full-size ones that you can transfer to the stock. Patterns for small parts can be enlarged on 4/4 graph paper (4 squares to the inch). For larger patterns, draw a grid of 1-inch squares on butcher paper, then sketch in the shape.

If you're making just one or two parts from the pattern, cut it out and affix it to the stock with a low-tack spray adhesive (available at art stores). For multiple parts of the same type, make a sturdy reusable pattern from stiff cardboard, ⅛-inch tempered hardboard (such as Masonite), or plastic laminate (such as Formica), from which you can trace the shape.

Finish. The finish we applied to the Adirondack Ensemble is actually the best outdoor finish: paint. The reason it is so good is that it covers and shields the wood from view. And thus from the sun.

Lovely, warm sunlight is remarkably destructive to bare wood. The heat bakes the moisture and resins out of the wood, and the ultraviolet (UV) rays discolor the wood and actually cause surface erosion. A clear coating like spar varnish deters the migration of moisture in and out of the wood, but it can't mitigate the harmful effects of ultraviolet radiation. In fact, the varnish itself is degraded by the ultraviolet radiation, which is the reason the varnish makers put ultraviolet absorbers (UVAs) in their products.

What really protects wood against UV degradation is shielding it from the sun. The pigment in paint does this.

According to researchers at the federal government's Forest Products Laboratory, the most durable outdoor finish is obtained by applying two coats of a high-quality acrylic latex paint over an oil-based primer. Oil-based paints are more impervious to moisture than latex paints, but they are less flexible. Regardless of how well it is sealed, wood swells and shrinks. The latex paint stretches and shrinks with the wood, while the oil-based coating eventually cracks. To prolong the life of the paint, the researchers recommend coating the wood with a water-repellent preservative before priming.

One last note on the finish. Knots in the wood you use will bleed through a painted finish. It may take a year or so, but it will happen. To prevent this, seal the knots with fresh shellac or prime the whole project with a pigmented shellac, such as Kilz or Bullseye.

All this takes a lot of time, but the time you invest now will come back to you with interest in years to come. A varnish or penetrating oil finish needs to be "refreshed" every couple of years. Your painted chair may not need recoating for ten years!

---

1. Cut and assemble the parts forming the lower frame assemblies. Start by cutting the legs and rails for both the chair and the ottoman from 5/4 stock. Take the dimensions for the legs from each *Side View* and lay out the pieces on the stock. Enlarge the rail patterns and sketch them on the stock. Use a band saw or saber saw to cut out the parts. Radius all the exposed edges using a router and a ¼-inch rounding-over bit.

Assemble the legs and rails with glue and 1⅝-inch screws, driving the screws through the rails into the legs. Be sure to make left and right assemblies (mirror images of each other). Line up the rails 1 inch back from the front edge of the legs. This setback provides for the thickness of the apron plus a ¼-inch reveal where it joins the legs.

Cut the front aprons from 1 × 6 boards. Enlarge the apron pattern, sketch it on the stock, and cut out the pieces. Attach the aprons to the front ends of the rails with glue and 2-inch screws. The edges of the leg should be ¼ inch proud of the faces of the aprons. Cut the back cleat and bevel it. Fasten it across the rails, 12 inches from the back end.

Finally, cut and attach the arm braces to the tops of the legs. Make sure the tops of the braces are perfectly flush with the tops of the legs.

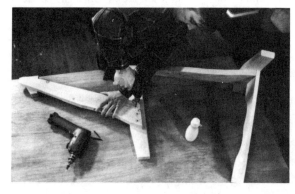

Assemble the legs and rails with glue and two or three 2-inch galvanized screws at each joint. Make sure the assemblies are mirror images, not duplicates.

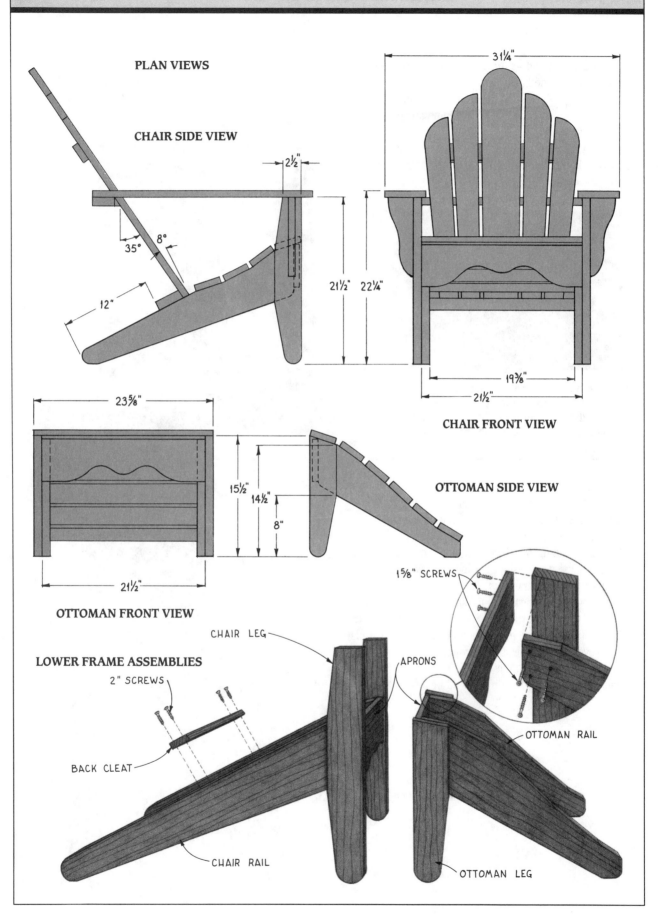

PLAN VIEWS

CHAIR SIDE VIEW

2½"

35° 8°

12"

21½" 22¼"

31¼"

19⅜"

21½"

CHAIR FRONT VIEW

23⅝"

15½" 14½"

8"

21½"

OTTOMAN FRONT VIEW

OTTOMAN SIDE VIEW

1⅝" SCREWS

LOWER FRAME ASSEMBLIES

CHAIR LEG

APRONS

2" SCREWS

BACK CLEAT

OTTOMAN RAIL

CHAIR RAIL

OTTOMAN LEG

2. Cut and assemble the arms and the back support. Cut the back support from 5/4 stock, and rip a 35-degree bevel along the front edge. Form 3½-inch-wide notches at each end by trimming away the bevel, as shown.

Cut the arms from 1 × 6 stock (use knot-free pieces, if possible), and rout ¼-inch radii all around the edges.

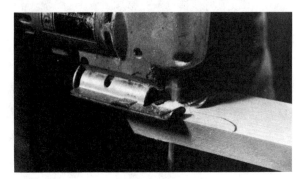

Shape the back support in stages. *Above:* Begin by notching the ends to remove the bevel. *Right:* After joining the back support to the arms, round off the ends of the support, using the arm's curve as a guide.

Glue and screw the arms to the back support, using 1¼-inch screws. Keep the curved ends of the arms flush with the ends of the back support and be sure the arms are 20½ inches apart at the front.

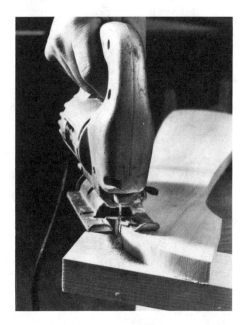

3. Start the back assembly. Enlarge the pattern for the center back slat, sketch it on the stock, then cut out the slat. Radius the edges with a router and a ¼-inch rounding-over bit. Then glue and screw the slat to the back cleat, using 1¼-inch screws. Be sure to center the slat on the cleat.

Now fasten the arm/back support assembly to the slat and the tops of the legs. You may want to temporarily clamp it in place and do a little measuring (or just plain eyeballing) to be sure it is where you want it before you actually fasten it. The slat should be centered on the back support, and the arms should be level.

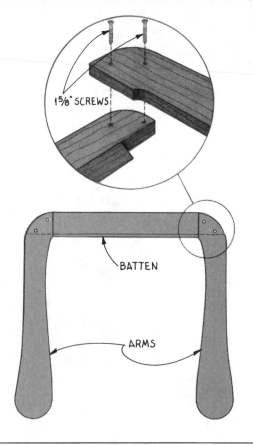

1⅝" SCREWS

BATTEN

ARMS

ARM/BACK SUPPORT ASSEMBLY

Aligning the arms and back support for assembly is easy, if a bit imprecise. Position the support on the arms and run a screw into each joint. Place a framing square next to an arm and the back support, and visually line up the pieces in relation to it. When you are satisfied that the arm and support are at right angles to each other, drive a second screw into the joint.

4. **Cut and install the back, seat, and otto-man slats.** The remaining back slats are cut from 1 × 4 stock. Radius the edges, then attach them to the back cleat and back support with glue and 1⅝-inch screws.

Enlarge the arm brace pattern and lay out two of the braces on 5/4 stock. Cut them out, radius the curved edges, and mount them against the arms and legs with glue and 2-inch screws.

Cut a batten and 10 seat slats. Radius all exposed edges, and attach these pieces to complete the chair and ottoman. Use 2-inch screws to attach the seat slats, 1¼-inch screws for the batten. Position the ottoman top slat so it caps the ends of the legs.

5. **Apply a finish.** Fill the screw holes with wood putty. Then sand, prime, and paint the chair and ottoman.

For the most durable finish, generously apply a water-repellent preservative to the sanded project. Allow this sealer to dry for as long as a week before shellacking the knots and priming the wood. Use an oil-based primer. After the primer dries, apply two coats of an exterior-grade latex paint. At each stage, pay special attention to the joints and to exposed end grain. Be sure these areas are thoroughly sealed.

TIP

Making screwheads "disappear" involves a combination of countersinking, puttying, and finish sanding. To start, countersink screws deeply enough to provide a foundation for the putty. We used a tapered pilot hole bit with an adjustable countersink to drill and countersink the screw holes before driving the screws. Immediately upon application, the putty should be just proud of the wood surface. The shrinkage of drying will reduce the bulge so you can quickly sand it flush with the wood surface. If you apply too little putty, you probably will have to add more, because it will shrink below the wood surface.

ADIRONDACK ENSEMBLE SIDE TABLE

A side table is a nearly essential component of the Adirondack Ensemble. The chair's arms *are* wide enough to accommodate a tall glass, but what will you do with that tray of snacks and ice-cold beverage pitcher? If you are making a brace of chairs and the settee, by all means, make a matching side table or two.

The table picks up the chair's slat lines for its tabletop slats. The table's aprons borrow the profile of the chair apron, and, of course, the leg profiles echo those of the chair. Made of the same materials, using the same joinery, the table is a natural companion to the chair and settee.

SHOPPING LIST

LUMBER

2 pcs. 1 × 4 × 8' #2 white pine
1 pc. 1 × 3 × 10' #2 white pine

HARDWARE AND SUPPLIES

1 box #6 × 1¼" galvanized drywall-type screws
1 box #6 × 1⅝" galvanized drywall-type screws
1 box #6 × 2" galvanized drywall-type screws
Wood putty
Resorcinol glue

FINISH

Exterior paint or clear finish of your choice

CUTTING LIST

PIECE	NUMBER	THICKNESS	WIDTH	LENGTH	MATERIAL
Table legs	4	¾"	3½"	17¼"	1 × 4 pine
Side aprons	2	¾"	3½"	18"	1 × 4 pine
End aprons	2	¾"	3½"	11¾"	1 × 4 pine
Battens	3	¾"	1½"	10¼"	1 × 4 pine
Center top slat	1	¾"	3½"	33½"	1 × 4 pine
Long top slats	2	¾"	2½"	30"	1 × 3 pine
Short top slats	2	¾"	2½"	25"	1 × 3 pine

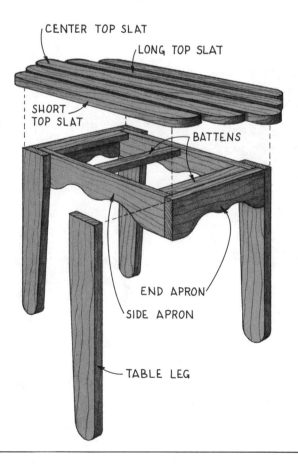

CENTER TOP SLAT
LONG TOP SLAT
SHORT TOP SLAT
BATTENS
END APRON
SIDE APRON
TABLE LEG

Builder's Notes

A companion project to this chapter's chair with otto-man and settee, the side table is constructed with the same materials and uses the same tools and techniques as its companion projects. If you are building only this project from the ensemble, then by all means read the "Builder's Notes" accompanying the Adirondack Chair with Ottoman project on page 78.

TOOL LIST

Drill
    Countersink bit
    Pilot hole bit
Paintbrush
Router
    ¼" rounding-over bit
Saber saw
Sander(s)

Sandpaper
Saw for crosscutting
Saw for ripping
Sawhorses
Screwdriver
Tack cloth
Tape measure
Try square

CUTTING DIAGRAM

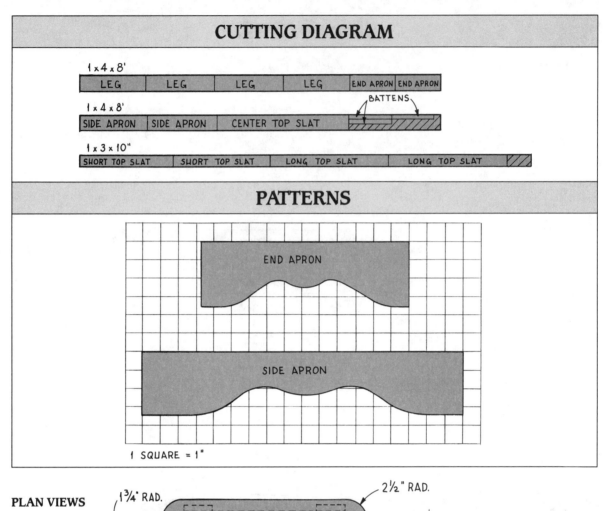

1 x 4 x 8'

| LEG | LEG | LEG | LEG | END APRON | END APRON |

1 x 4 x 8'

| SIDE APRON | SIDE APRON | CENTER TOP SLAT | BATTENS |

1 x 3 x 10"

| SHORT TOP SLAT | SHORT TOP SLAT | LONG TOP SLAT | LONG TOP SLAT |

PATTERNS

END APRON

SIDE APRON

1 SQUARE = 1"

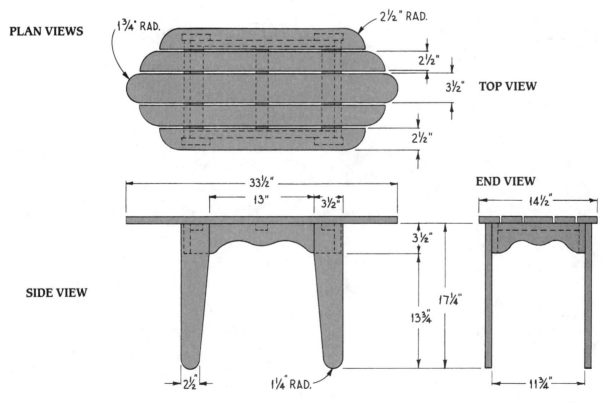

PLAN VIEWS

1¾" RAD.

2½" RAD.

2½"

3½" **TOP VIEW**

2½"

SIDE VIEW

33½"

13"

3½"

3½"

17¼"

13¾"

2½"

1¼" RAD.

END VIEW

14½"

11¾"

1. Cut out and assemble the legs and side aprons for the table. Lay out the legs using the dimensions shown on the *Side View.* Note that they are tapered along one edge only, and their bottoms are rounded. Enlarge the side apron pattern and sketch it on the stock. Using a band saw or saber saw, cut out these parts. With a router and a ¼-inch rounding-over bit, radius all exposed edges.

Glue and screw the parts together, forming two U-shaped frames. Use 1¼-inch screws. The legs overlay the aprons. Keep the ends of the aprons 1 inch back from the outside edges of the legs.

TIP

It's a good idea to have two drill-drivers close at hand when assembling this project. Equip one with a pilot hole bit, which is a special combination bit that bores and countersinks a tapered pilot hole in one operation. Equip the other with a screwdriver bit. During assembly, line up the two (glued) pieces to be joined, holding them tightly in position with one hand. Pick up the drill with the other hand and bore the pilot hole. Still holding the workpieces, set down the drill, pick up the driver, and drive the screw.

---

2. Complete the leg/apron assembly. Enlarge the end apron pattern and sketch it on the stock. Cut out the aprons, radius the edges, then glue and screw them to the ends of the side aprons with 2-inch screws, thus joining the two assemblies made in the previous step.

Cut three battens. Using 1⅝-inch screws, attach one to the inside of each end apron. The third batten is installed in the next step.

---

3. Make and install the top. Cut out the table-top slats, and round the ends as shown in the Top View. Arrange them facedown on a flat surface. Apply glue to the top surfaces of the leg/apron assembly, turn it upside down, and position it carefully on the slats. Drive 1¼-inch screws through the battens and into the slats. Glue and screw the third batten across the middle of the slats.

---

4. Apply a finish. Fill the screw holes with wood putty. Then sand, prime, and paint the table a color that will go well with your favorite set of tall glasses.

TIP

Before you paint your Adirondack furniture, be sure to prime knots with shellac or a pigmented shellac. If you don't, they will bleed through any paint you apply, blemishing your finished project.

ADIRONDACK ENSEMBLE SETTEE

This settee makes a congenial addition to the basic Adirondack chair/ottoman/table set. It seats two comfortably and generally encourages intimacy—that is, if both occupants can agree to share the center armrest.

If you're making the chair, it won't require much more work to build the settee because it's really just two chairs joined by a center leg/arm assembly and continu-ous seat slats and back support. Most of the remaining components are exactly the same as those used for the chair, so you can use the same patterns for both projects.

The ottoman for the chair also fits one side of the settee, so you might opt to make another pair of them—and two more side tables, if you're feeling especially ambitious.

SHOPPING LIST

LUMBER

1 pc. 5/4 × 6 × 12' #2 pine
1 pc. 5/4 × 4 × 16' #2 pine
1 pc. 1 × 6 × 12' #2 pine*
1 pc. 1 × 6 × 6' #2 pine
1 pc. 1 × 4 × 10' #2 pine
1 pc. 1 × 4 × 12' #2 pine
1 pc. 1 × 4 × 14' #2 pine
1 pc. 1 × 3 × 4' #2 pine

HARDWARE AND SUPPLIES

1 box #6 × 1¼" galvanized drywall-type screws
1 box #6 × 1⅝" galvanized drywall-type screws
1 box #6 × 2" galvanized drywall-type screws
Wood putty
Resorcinol glue

FINISH

Exterior paint or clear finish of your choice

*Try to get one with two clear 30" lengths from which to cut the arms.

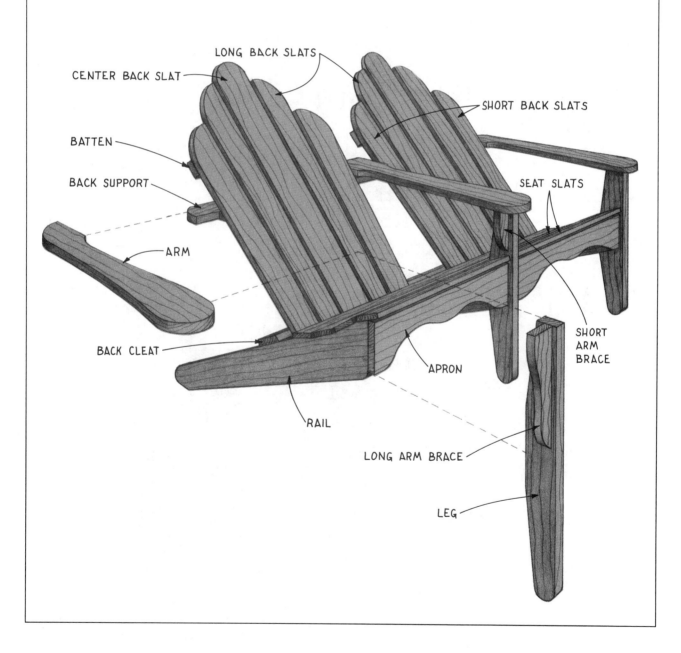

CUTTING LIST

PIECE	NUMBER	THICKNESS	WIDTH	LENGTH	MATERIAL
Rails*	4	1¹⁄₁₆"	5½"	31½"	5/4 × 6 pine
Legs*	3	1¹⁄₁₆"	3½"	21½"	5/4 × 4 pine
Aprons*	2	¾"	5½"	21½"	1 × 6 pine
Back cleat	1	1¹⁄₁₆"	3½"	44"	5/4 × 4 pine
Back support	1	1¹⁄₆"	5½"	51"	5/4 × 4 pine
Arms*	3	¾"	5½"	29"	1 × 6 pine†
Center back slats*	2	¾"	5½"	35½"	1 × 6 pine
Long back slats*	4	¾"	3½"	33"	1 × 4 pine
Short back slats*	4	¾"	3½"	29½"	1 × 4 pine
Long arm braces*	2	1¹⁄₁₆"	3"	10"	5/4 × 4 pine
Short arm braces	2	1¹⁄₁₆"	3"	5"	5/4 × 4 pine
Battens*	2	¾"	2½"	20"	1 × 3 pine
Seat slats	4	¾"	3½"	44"	1 × 4 pine

*Piece identical to that on Adirondack Chair
†Cut from knot-free section, if possible.

PATTERNS

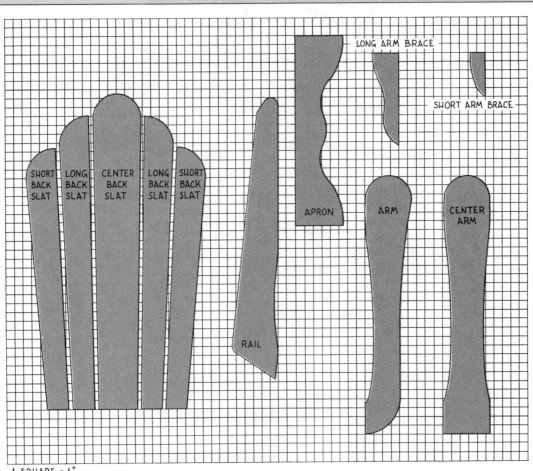

1 SQUARE = 1"

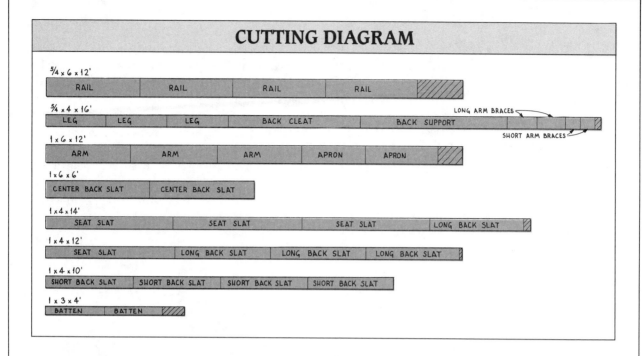

CUTTING DIAGRAM

Builder's Notes

A companion project to this chapter's chair with ottoman and side table, the settee is constructed with the same materials and uses the same tools and techniques as its companion projects. If you are building only this project from the ensemble, then by all means read the "Builder's Notes" accompanying the Adirondack Chair with Ottoman project on page 78.

---

1. Cut and assemble the parts for the leg/rail assemblies. Cut the three legs and the four rails for the leg/rail assemblies. To lay out the rails, enlarge the pattern. To lay out the legs, use the dimensions shown in the *Side View.* Use a band saw or saber saw to cut out the parts. Rout a ¼-inch radius on all the exposed edges using a router and a ¼-inch rounding-over bit.

To make the center leg/rail assembly, attach a rail to each side of one of the legs. During assembly, use a scrap of 5/4 stock as a temporary spacer to keep the rear ends of the rails apart (see photo). Glue and screw the rails onto the legs from both sides, using three or four 2-inch screws on each side. Make left- and right-hand leg assemblies next, attaching the legs to the rails with glue and 1⅝-inch screws. Drive the screws through the

rails into the legs. On all assemblies, position the front end of the rails 1 inch back from the front edge of the legs. This setback provides for the thickness of the aprons plus a ¼-inch reveal where they join the legs.

Next, enlarge the patterns for the aprons, transfer them to the stock, and cut out these pieces. Use glue and 2-inch screws to attach the aprons to the front ends of

The center leg/rail assembly is one of the design components used to join two "chairs" to make one settee. Attach a rail to each side of the center leg to form this component. Use a scrap of 5/4 stock as a temporary spacer to help align the rails during assembly.

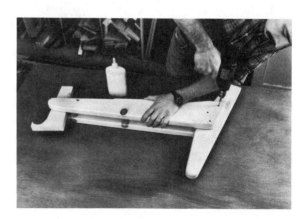

the rails, thus joining the three leg assemblies at the front. Make sure the top edges of the aprons are flush with the top edges of the rails.

Now, cut the back cleat to length and rip an 8-degree bevel along the front edge. Attach the cleat across the top of the rails, 12 inches from the back end. Drive screws through the cleat into the outside rails first, then carefully align the middle rail assembly so it is properly centered before fastening the cleat to it. Use glue and 1⅝-inch screws.

To complete the assembly, enlarge the patterns for the arm braces, transfer them to the stock, and cut out these pieces. Fasten the arm braces to the legs with glue and 2-inch screws. Make sure the tops of the braces are flush with the tops of the legs.

LOWER FRAME ASSEMBLY

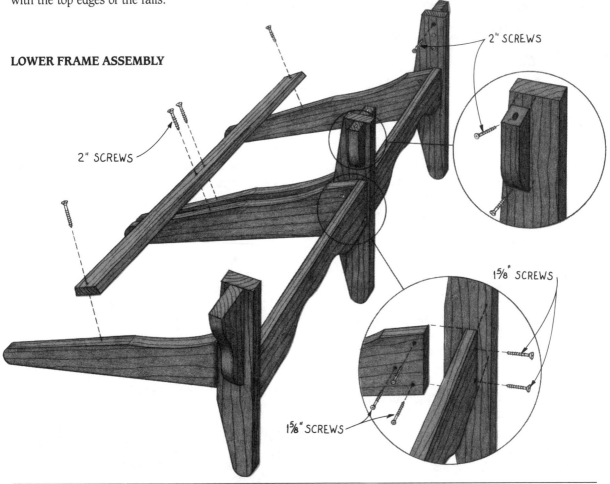

2" SCREWS

2" SCREWS

1⅝" SCREWS

1⅝" SCREWS

2. Cut and assemble the arms and back support. Cut the back support to length and rip a 35-degree bevel along the front edge. With a saber saw, trim away 3½ inches of the bevel at each end of the support, forming notches, as shown in the *Arm/Back Support Assembly* drawing.

Next, lay out and cut the left, right, and center arms (from clear, knot-free stock, if possible). Rout a ¼-inch radius around the exposed edges on both sides of each piece.

Join the arms to the back support with glue and 1⅝-inch screws. Lay out the pieces, as shown in the

PLAN VIEWS

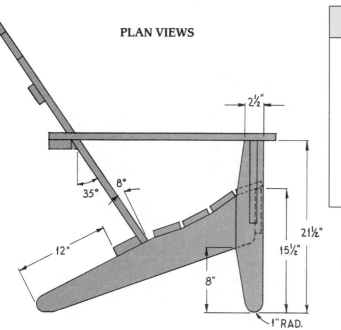

SIDE VIEW

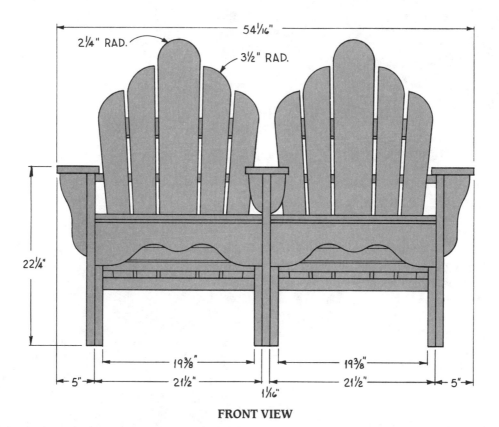

FRONT VIEW

Arm/Back Support Assembly drawing. Use a framing square to aid in visual alignment when joining the outer arms to the back support (see step 2 of the Adirondack Chair with Ottoman project on page 82). After the outer arms are attached, use two tape measures, as shown in the photo, to position the center arm equidistant between the outer arms.

Finally, use a saber saw to trim the edges of the back support to the same curve as that on the arms (see step 3 of the Adirondack Chair with Ottoman directions).

ARM/BACK SUPPORT ASSEMBLY

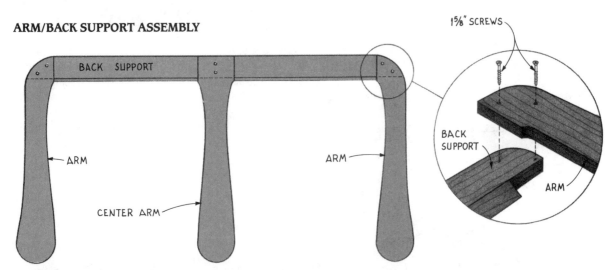

After the two outer arms are fastened in place, use two tape measures, as shown, to align the center arm between the outer ones. When the center arm is an equal distance from each of the outer arms—you'll have the same measurement on both tapes—drive a couple of screws through the support into the arm to secure it.

3. **Attach the center slats to the leg/rail assembly.** Enlarge the pattern for the center back slats, lay out two center back slats, then cut them out. Radius the edges with a router and a ¼-inch rounding-over bit.

Fasten each slat to the back cleat with a couple of 2-inch screws. Make sure each slat is centered between its rails and perpendicular to the cleat (use a framing square to aid in vertical alignment, if necessary).

Holding a center slat in position while you drill pilot holes and drive screws may seem more difficult than it is. Rest the meat of the slat on your shoulder and pinch the base against the cleat with one hand, while you operate a drill with the other. Aligning the butt edge of the slat flush with the edge of the cleat *should* ensure that the slat is perpendicular.

4. **Fasten the arm/back support assembly to the slats and the tops of the legs.** Set the arm/back support assembly in position. Make sure the arms are level (to establish this, simply set a level on an arm and watch the bubble while you move the back support up and down), then join the slats to the back support with glue and 1⅝-inch screws. Center the fronts of the arms on the tops of the legs and attach them to the legs and the arm support brackets with glue and 2-inch screws.

Use two spring clamps as an extra set of hands while leveling the arm/back support assembly. Roughly position the arms on the legs, then use a level to determine where the back support will attach to the center slats to ensure perfectly level arms. Clip a spring clamp on each slat and rest the assembly on them as you fine-tune the fit and complete the installation.

5. **Cut and install the back and seat slats.** Enlarge the patterns for the remaining back slats, laying out four slats from each pattern. Unlike the center slat, which has two tapered sides, only one side of these slats is tapered. Radius the edges, then attach them to the back cleat and back support with glue and 1⅝-inch screws.

Next, cut the seat slats and two battens. Use 2-inch screws to attach the slats to the leg/rail assembly and 1¼-inch screws to attach the battens to the slats.

6. **Apply a finish.** Fill the screw holes with wood putty. Then sand, prime, and apply the finish of your choice. After the finish dries, move the settee to a pleasant spot in the yard and invite a friend or relative to sit with you.

RUSH-SEATED PORCH ROCKER

Straight from America's Front Porch

Rocking on the porch. A traditional American pastime. In traditional *American* communities, the communities of *The Music Man* and *American Gothic* and Thomas Hart Benton. In scattered rural enclaves and on farms across the heartland: The hay's all stacked, the corn's growing noisily, and the porch rocker creaks contentedly. In bustling towns, wherever there are single houses with

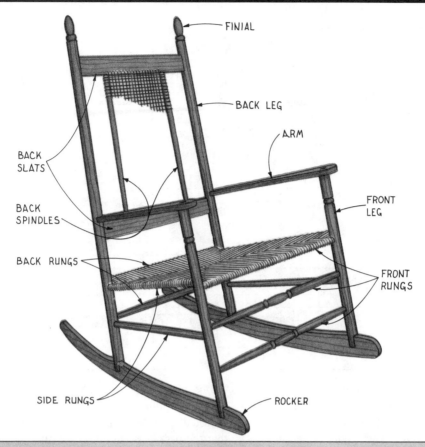

FINIAL

BACK LEG

ARM

FRONT LEG

FRONT RUNGS

BACK SLATS

BACK SPINDLES

BACK RUNGS

SIDE RUNGS

ROCKER

SHOPPING LIST

LUMBER

2 pcs. 1⅜″ dia. × 40″ oak dowel*
8¼ bd. ft. 8/4 oak

HARDWARE AND SUPPLIES

2 pcs. #6 × 3″ galvanized drywall-type screws
4′ mason's cord (or comparable string)
6 lb. ⁶⁄₃₂″ fiber rush*

HARDWARE AND SUPPLIES—CONTINUED

Resorcinol glue
Transparent tape

FINISH

Penetrating oil finish for rush seat and backrest
Clear exterior finish for wood

*Available via mail-order from Constantine's,
2050 Eastchester Road, Bronx, NY 10461.

CUTTING LIST

PIECE	NUMBER	THICKNESS	WIDTH	LENGTH	MATERIAL
Back legs	2	1⅜″ dia.		39″	Oak dowel
Front legs	2	1½″	1½″	20¼″	Oak
Front rungs	3	1″	1″	23″	Oak
Back/side rungs	6	1″	1″	18″	Oak
Finials	2	1⅜″	1⅜″	4″	Oak
Back slats	2	1½″	2½″	18″	Oak
Arms	2	¾″	3½″	20½″	Oak
Rockers	2	¾″	6″	35″	Oak
Back spindles	2	¾″	¾″	19″	Oak

PATTERNS

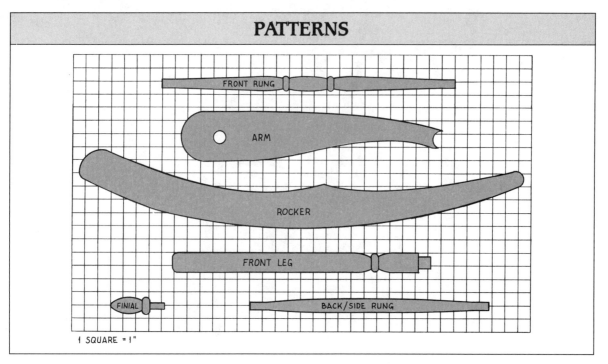

FRONT RUNG

ARM

ROCKER

FRONT LEG

FINIAL

BACK/SIDE RUNG

1 SQUARE = 1"

porches, sheltering trees, and a little street activity—kids running to the playground, folks walking to the corner store, families out for a Sunday stroll. There you sit and rock and quietly talk, pawing idly at the still air with a fan.

Okay, so here's a rocker you can build yourself. It's the traditional porch rocker, with turned legs, spindles, and rungs; a woven seat and back; and flat armrests. The square, angular design truly belies the rocker's comfort: The woven rush seat and back provide firm support, yet have more "give" than solid wood or wood slats. The low, wide armrests add to the rocker's comfort, enabling you to read, knit, or do other handwork without interference.

Builder's Notes

This rocker is one of the more advanced projects in this book. The instructions assume you have a well-equipped shop, with a table saw, drill press, band saw, and lathe, and the basic know-how to use them. The project will test your weaving skills, too.

Materials. You can use practically any hardwood for the rocker. A dense wood, such as oak, ash, or maple, is best for the rockers, because the bottom edges will need to withstand wear and abrasion.

In choosing materials, a pivotal part of the rocker is the back leg. Few home woodshop lathes—and that includes the one in our shop—have the capacity to turn

the 40-inch-long back legs. To circumvent this problem, we used manufactured 1⅜-inch by 40-inch dowels, purchased through the mail from Constantine's. (You'll note that the back legs are untapered and unembellished.) Because the dowels we bought were red oak, we used this wood for most of the rocker.

As with all hardwoods, oak isn't stocked at every lumberyard and it isn't available in predictable sizes. Thicknesses are standardized, but not widths and lengths. With a band saw—and you at least need access to one to make this project—you can rough-cut all the pieces you

TOOL LIST

Band clamps	Paintbrush
Band saw	Sander(s)
Bar clamps	Sandpaper
Bench vise	Sawhorses
Calipers	Scissors
Chisel	Screwdriver
Dividers	Spring clamps
Drill	Table saw
Pilot hole bit	Tack cloth
Drill press	Tape measure
Various-size drill bits	Trammel
Various-size Forstner bits	Try square
Framing square	Turning chisels
Lathe	

need for the rocker from an 8/4 (eight-quarter) plank. Dressed, the plank will be 1¾ inches thick, sufficient to yield the thickest parts (the legs and back slats). And using a band saw, you can easily resaw sections of the plank into thinner pieces to get the 1-inch square billets for the rungs, as well as the ¾-inch-thick rockers and arms.

The "Shopping List" specifies the purchase of 8¼ board feet of 8/4 oak. With hardwoods, you must keep the dimensions of the necessary parts in mind when you shop. A board might contain the requisite number of board feet without having the correct dimensions to give you the parts you need. For example, a 12-foot-long oak 8/4 × 4, should you find one, contains 8 board feet—almost enough for the rocker. But you wouldn't be able to cut the 6-inch-wide rockers from this board, and they represent almost 40 percent of your lumber need.

The seat and back of the rocker are woven of fiber rush. Fiber rush is made from a tough grade of paper twisted into a strand to simulate natural rush. It is usually sold in coils by the pound, rather than by length, in strand widths designated 3/32 inch, 4/32 inch, 5/32 inch, and 6/32 inch. You'll need approximately 6 pounds of 6/32-inch rush to do the back and seat of the rocker. We purchased the fiber rush for the seat and back from Constantine's.

Tools and techniques. To make the rocker just as shown, you need a lathe and lathe tools, along with basic spindle-turning skills. Great proficiency isn't required, since the ornamentation is pretty modest. In fact, this is a very good project for the beginning turner.

To cut the curved back slats, you must have (or have access to) a band saw. No other tool will do. You can, however, cut the arms with a saber saw.

To clamp the rocker, perhaps the easiest clamps to use are band clamps. Bar or pipe clamps work, but you need to use cauls with them to avoid marring the wood. If you do use pipe or bar clamps, cut V-shaped grooves into them to give them the best purchase on the curved surfaces of the legs and rungs.

Holes for the rungs are best bored on a drill press. Use Forstner bits to bore the required holes. You'll notice that the seat is wider at the front than at the back, which means that the rungs are not 90 degrees to each other where they join the legs. You'll want to make a "dogleg" fixture to aid in positioning the holes. The details for making the fixture are shown in step 6.

Weaving rush seats is a time-honored craft that takes a bit of practice to master. If this is your first shot at it, though, you can still expect reasonably good results for this project if you pay close attention to the instructions and take your time.

Weaving the rush seat and back requires no specialized tools or equipment; after weaving each course, you'll need to pack it tight against the previous one with a hammer and wood block. Weaving will take your full concentration: Read the directions carefully, making sure you fully understand the method before you start. The secret to a firm seat and back lies in keeping the strands taut as you weave and pack each course.

---

1. Cut all parts to size. Rip and crosscut all the parts for the rocker to the sizes specified by the "Cutting List." It helps if you label each part so you don't get them mixed up. Pieces for the arms and rockers should be milled to exact thickness.

---

2. Turn the rungs, front legs, and finials. Because turning on a lathe creates a lot of shavings, it's best to make all the turned parts at once and clean up just one mess afterward.

One by one, mount the billets for the front legs, rungs, and back spindles, as shown in the photos on page 296. Use the patterns as guides in turning the parts. When making the rungs and back spindles, turn the tenons first, then turn the body of the part to a pleasing curve that blends into the tenon.

The "Cutting List" specifies the exact lengths for the rungs, front legs, and back spindles. To minimize "whipping," it's best to keep the turnings as short as possible. You can do this by cutting the billets to the exact length. Where the turning attaches to the spur center on the headstock, leave a short portion of the tenon unturned. (A cone center on the tailstock enables you to turn all the way to the end). After removing the piece from the lathe, trim these ends with a chisel or pocketknife.

To mount billets for the various turned pieces, you must locate the center point on each end. *Left:* Scribe diagonals to do this. Kerf one end on the diagonal marks so you can attach the billet to the headstock.

Right: Then, as you adjust the lathe's tailstock to "capture" the billet, make sure its point penetrates the center point.

Left: To monitor your progress during turning operations, use calipers. Set the calipers to, for example, the diameter of the spindle's tenon. Begin the cut at the shoulder of the tenon. Periodically interrrupt your cutting to fit the calipers to the cut, as shown. When the calipers just drop over the cut, you have achieved the correct diameter. Turn the rest of the tenon in a series of similar cuts.

Right: After the tenons on each end are cut, begin to shape the rung or spindle profile. Work from the ends toward the middle, rounding the billet. Taper the piece from the middle to blend into the tenons.

3. **Cut out the back slats.** Rather than steam and bend the back slats to shape, we used a band saw to cut the curved slats.

Begin with stock about 1½ inches thick and about 2½ inches wide. Use a string compass or trammel to scribe the outer arc—it has a 50-inch radius—on the edge of the stock. Cut freehand along the line on the band saw. Next, set a pencil compass or dividers to ¾ inch and mark a parallel arc on the stock, using the newly cut edge as a guide. Then make the second cut.

Before leaving the band saw, use it to cut the tenons on the ends of the slats, as shown on the *Back Slat Layout.*

BACK SLAT LAYOUT

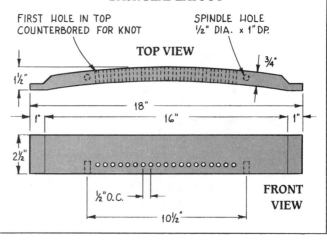

FIRST HOLE IN TOP
COUNTERBORED FOR KNOT

SPINDLE HOLE
½" DIA. x 1" DP.

TOP VIEW

1½"

¾"

18"

16"

1"

1"

2½"

FRONT VIEW

½" O.C.

10½"

TIP

If you are skeptical about cutting the second face of the back slat freehand, use a pivot block to guide the cut. The block supports the narrow stock vertically, plus it ensures that the thickness of the piece will be uniform.

The pivot point of the block consists of two 45-degree cuts; the height of the block should equal the thickness of the board you'll be cutting. After drawing the cutting line on the stock, cut about 1 inch along the line. Then turn off the saw and clamp the block to the saw table, with its point against the stock directly opposite the blade. Restart the saw and complete the cut. Advance the workpiece with one hand, while guiding it against the pivot block with the other. Keep your hands clear of the blade, even when it's buried in the stock.

Note that the block can't be used for guiding the first arc, nor can it be used for cutting curved parts that vary in width, such as the rockers.

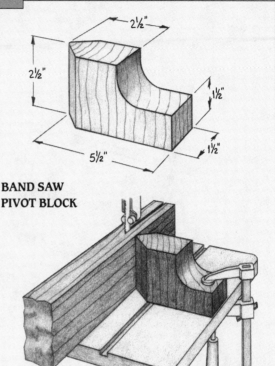

BAND SAW PIVOT BLOCK

4. **Drill holes in the back slats for the back spindles and rush.** Measure and mark the hole locations for the back spindles, as shown on the *Back Slat Layout.* Drill ½-inch-diameter holes 1 inch deep. Clamp the workpiece to your bench or drill press table to steady it while drilling.

The holes along the bottom edge of the top slat and the top edge of the bottom slat are used to thread the warp strands for the rush back. Decide which slat will be the top, and which the bottom, and drill the holes accordingly. As shown in the drawing, there are 19 holes in each slat, ¼ inch in diameter, spaced ½ inch apart. Counterbore the first hole on the left side of the top slat to ½ inch diameter and ¼ inch deep from the back side of the slat. This provides a recess to help conceal the knot you will tie in the rush warp at its starting point.

5. **Notch the front and back legs for the rockers.** As indicated in the *Side View,* the bottoms of the front and back legs are notched so they fit over the rockers. Since the rockers will be ¾ inch thick, make the notches ¾ inch wide. The bottoms of the notches are perpendicular to the length of the legs. Mark the notch locations and cut them on the band saw, making them 1½ inches deep.

6. **Mortise the legs for the back slats and rungs.** This is a key step in building the rocker. Each of the four legs has holes drilled in two planes, and all the holes must be aligned accurately if you are going to be able to assemble the legs, rungs, and slats. If you've never done this before, it can seem tricky, but the simple dogleg fixture we used makes the alignment operation easy.

PLAN VIEWS

SIDE VIEW

FRONT VIEW

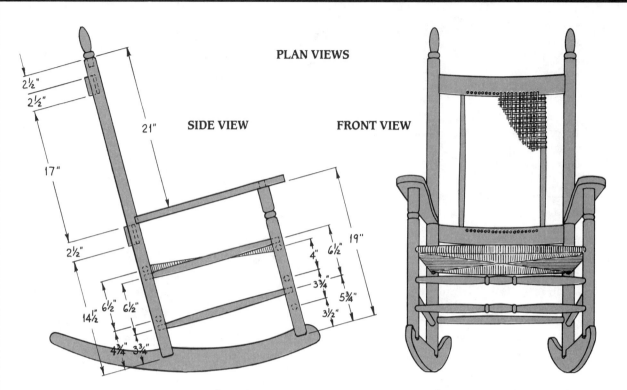

TOP VIEW

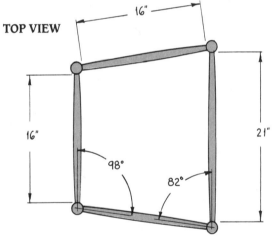

Lay out the mortises first. Use a square to mark the locations on the front and back legs for the rung mortises and the back slat mortises. Make sure you position the holes for mirror-image left and right legs.

To steady the turned legs for drilling, you'll need a V-block, such as you would use when drilling any cylindrical object. If you don't already have such a block, set your table saw or radial arm saw to make a bevel rip, then cut a V-groove about an inch wide in a scrap of 2 × 4 about 2 feet long. Clamp (or fasten temporarily with bolts) the V-block to the drill press table with the center of the groove directly beneath the bit.

To align the legs in the V-block so the axis of each hole will be correct, make the fixture shown in the *Dogleg*

Fixture Detail. Fit the fixture into the rocker notch in the leg and sight-align it with either the bit or the drill press table, depending upon which holes you are boring.

For example, to drill the round mortises for the front rungs in the front legs, fit the long leg of the fixture into the rocker notch. The mark for one of the mortises should be directly under the bit. Sight along the leg, aligning the fixture with the drill bit, rolling the leg slightly in the V-block as necessary to achieve the proper alignment. When the fixture is parallel with the bit, drill your hole. Each time you shift the leg to line up the next mark under the bit, recheck your alignment against the fixture.

This alignment setup is used for the front rung mortises (in the front legs), as well as the back rung and back slat mortises (in the back legs). To drill the side rung mortises in both the front and back legs, a different alignment setup is used.

DOGLEG FIXTURE DETAIL

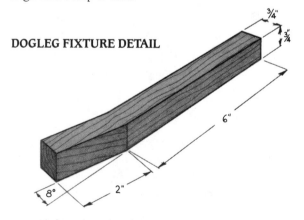

For these holes, fit the short leg of the fixture in the rocker notch, *then align the long leg parallel to the drill press table,* as shown in the photos. To make the alignment easier, cut a short 2 × 4 block and set it next to the V-block. Rotate the leg until the fixture is parallel to the block. (It will virtually rest on the block.) The kink in the fixture will position the leg to give you the correct axis for the side rungs in relation to the holes you drilled for the front or back rungs.

Drill the mortises with a Forstner bit, which yields a clean, flat-bottomed hole. The rung mortises, of course, are each a single hole. To make a slat mortise, drill a series of overlapping holes to rough it out, then use a chisel to square it up. Finally, drill a hole in the top of each back leg for the finials.

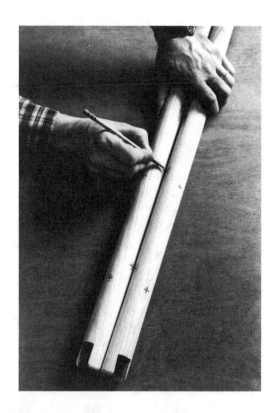

Right: Make sure you lay out the back slat mortises and rung holes to create left and right legs (mirror images) at front and back, rather than making identical parts. Perhaps the best way to do this is to mark one leg, then place the second beside it and transfer the position marks.

Cut four mortises for the back slats, two in each back leg. To do this, lay out each mortise, marking the length and width. *Far left:* Set the leg in the V-block, align it using the dogleg fixture, and drill a series of overlapping holes to excavate the bulk of the waste from the mortise. *Left:* Use a chisel to square the sides of the mortise.

Far left: To drill the mortises for the front and back rungs and the slats, fit the long leg of the dogleg fixture into the rocker notch, as shown. With the leg in the V-block, sight along the leg, aligning the dogleg fixture parallel to the drill bit, thereby rotating the leg into the proper alignment for drilling. *Left:* Align the leg for drilling the side rung mortises by switching the fixture so its short leg is in the rocker notch and its long leg is cocked to the side. Rotate the rocker leg so the fixture's long leg is parallel to the table; a scrap block set on the table makes the alignment easier to establish.

7. Assemble the back spindles and the back slats. Apply glue to the ends of the two back spindles and to the sockets in the back slats. Fit the parts together. When clamping them, lay the assembly facedown on a flat surface to avoid twisting it. After the glue dries, sand and finish the assembly, because it's easier to do now than after you've woven the rush back. Be sure you don't apply finish to the tenons, however, since these get glued into the mortises in the legs.

---

8. Weave the rush back. It is a lot easier to weave the back before it is joined to the rocker itself. Clamp it in a vise and pull up a chair to it. It will take a lot of time, so you might as well be as comfortable as possible.

Start by setting up the back assembly for weaving after its finish dries. Secure it upright in a bench vise, sandwiching the bottom slat between two pads of styrene material to compensate for the curvature of the slat and to protect the finish. Make sure the holes for the rush are exposed.

Thread the warp; this is the set of vertical strands. Cut a 50-foot strand of rush, which should be long enough to both thread the warp and start the weave. Feed one end of the rush through the first hole (with the counterbore), tie a knot in it, then pull it back so the knot settles into the counterbore. Thread the free end of the rush through the remaining holes, as shown in *Threading the Warp.* Make sure each loop is taut. After you complete the warp, start right in on the weave.

Follow the *Weaving Sequence* to make the diamond pattern we used for the back. This pattern requires you to alternate the over-under weave with each course.

After weaving each course, pack it tight. Without a strand above it, the course will tend to pop up the warp strands, pushing the weave away from the previous course. Use a scrap of hardwood, no more than a half-inch thick, to press down on the weave between each warp. To further tighten the weave, tap the stick with a hammer. (What you are really doing is packing the previous course, for the topmost weave will always pop up along the warp, no matter what you do.)

Initially, you will be able to thread the strand, also called the "weaver," over and under all the strands making up the warp. You pull the excess through easily, give the rush a sharp tug to pull it snug, then pack with the stick. But as you near completion, the warp will have so little "give" that you'll be reduced to threading the weaver over or under a single strand, then pulling through the excess, then threading it over another single warp strand, and so forth. At this point, you want to be working with a pretty short weaver. Not only is the

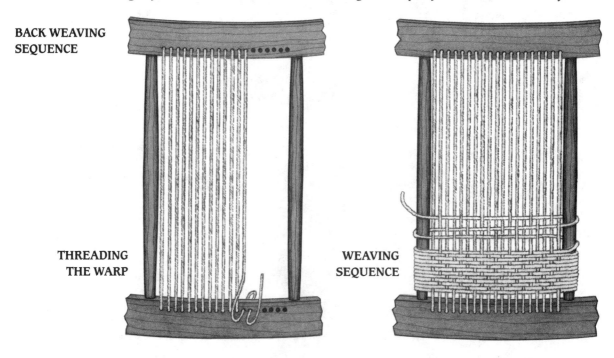

BACK WEAVING SEQUENCE

THREADING THE WARP

WEAVING SEQUENCE

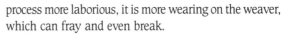

process more laborious, it is more wearing on the weaver, which can fray and even break.

Tie off the weave by wrapping the free end around the spindle for the last time and working it into the weave. You don't want to knot the rush and leave a lump to spoil the appearance of the weaving.

Left: Here's the basic setup for weaving the rush backrest. The back assembly is held firmly by the vise. The work area is free of clutter, the worker is comfortably seated.

Below left: Weaving one course for the back is a matter of looping the free end of the weaver around the spindle, then threading it over and under the warp strands in the required sequence, as shown. Then pull the excess through, yanking the weaver as taut as you can. Snug the weaver as tightly as possible against the previous course using your packing stick. *Below right:* Then pack the previous course, using the stick and a hammer. At each warp strand, fit the tip of the stick against the weaver and give the stick a rap.

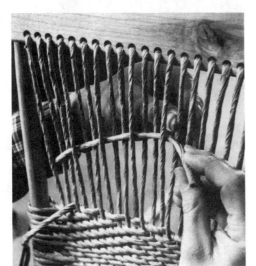

Above left: Fiber rush is made of a tough paper twisted into a strand to simulate natural rush. If you untwist and spread open the strand, you'll have a strip of paper 4 to 5 inches wide, as shown. *Above center:* To splice two strands together, untwist the ends of both the weaver and the new strand. With scissors, cut the ends at an angle, then tape them together with ordinary cellophane tape. Fold the splice with the tape inside, then fold again to ensure all the tape is concealed inside. *Above right:* Finally, carefully twist the splice, tightening it to blend into the strand.

9. **Assemble the back assembly, the legs, and the rungs.** Glue and clamp the woven back assembly between the back legs. Then, lay out the front rungs and front legs on a flat surface and glue and clamp them together. When making both assemblies, use a framing square to make sure they're clamped square. After the glue dries, connect the front leg assembly to the back leg assembly by installing the side rungs. Do not install the arms or rockers at this time.

TIP

When weaving the back and the seat, it's best to work with no more than 30 feet of rush at a time. If the strands are much longer, they'll be too unwieldy to work with; if much shorter, you'll end up making too many splices.

10. **Weave the seat.** Sand and finish the unfinished parts of the assembly you just made. When the finish dries, weave the rush seat.

The weaving sequence is a lot easier to show than it is to describe with words. The weaver winds over and under and around and over and under and . . . But you get the idea. Study both the photos and the *Seat Weaving Sequence* before you start. It is a lot easier than it sounds.

To start, you need to square up the seat opening—it's wider at the front than the back. You do this by filling the front corners. Tie two large loops of mason's twine to the back rung, then tie the end of the first strand of rush to one of them. Until you've squared off the opening, weave from one string loop across the front only (not across the back) to the other loop, then back again. To keep too many courses from bunching up in one loop,

Weaving the rocker seat is a matter of looping a continuous strand of rush in sequence around the rocker's rungs and itself. *Top:* Pass the coil of rush over and under and around the rungs, playing out the strand loosely. To keep the previous courses from loosening while leaving your hands free to thread the new course, use a spring clamp to pinch the taut weaver against a rung. *Center:* The photo shows how the strand is looped around the front and side rungs and itself, knitting an attractive seat surface. *Bottom:* After threading the rush fully around the seat, go back around, pulling it tight, while carefully aligning the strand next to previous courses. Reset the spring clamp and repeat the process. Note that here you can splice strands of rush with knots, so long as you position them where they will be hidden inside the weave. (Note also that, after finishing the seat weaving, we decided it would have been easier to do if the arms hadn't been in the way, and if the work didn't rock unpredictably. Weave yours before installing the arms and the rockers.)

SEAT WEAVING SEQUENCE

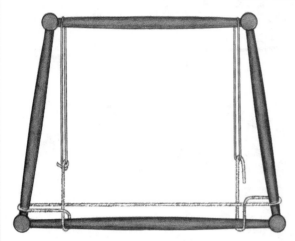 

make additional loops, each slightly shorter than the previous one, to distribute the strands evenly. The *Seat Weaving Sequence* shows the path of the weaver through a typical course.

After you've squared off the opening, you weave around all four sides to fill in the seat. To make the seat

really tight, you can use a stick and hammer, as you did when weaving the rocker back, to tighten each course against the previous one.

When you've finished weaving, "tuck" your loose end into the underside of the seat, making sure it's secure.

---

11. **Cut out and attach the arms.** Enlarge the arm pattern, and transfer it to the stock for the arms. Be sure to make mirror images, rather than two identical pieces. Cut out the basic shape of the arms on the band saw. Cut a radius in the back of the arms to fit around the back legs, as shown in the pattern, and test it for fit by positioning the arms against the leg. Make

any minor adjustments for a tight fit, then center the front of the arm over the front leg and mark the front hole location. Drill the front hole, then glue the front of the arm to the front and back legs. Drive a #6 × 3-inch galvanized drywall-type screw through the back leg into the end of the arm for additional strength.

---

12. **Cut out and attach the rockers.** Enlarge the rocker pattern, and use it to lay out two rockers on the working stock. Cut them out. Radius the edges of these rockers, except where they will be covered by the notched legs, with a router and a ¼-inch rounding-over

bit. Sand the rockers.

Glue the rockers into the notches in the legs. After the glue sets, drill a ¼-inch hole completely through the side of the leg at the notch (see the *Side View*) and drive a ¼-inch dowel into it to lock the rocker in place.

---

13. **Glue the finials on the back legs, sand all unfinished parts, and apply a finish.** After gluing on the finials, apply one coat of finish to all the unfinished parts of the rocker. Then, lightly sand the finished rocker with a fine-grit paper and apply a second coat of finish

to the entire project. On the rush seat and back, use a penetrating oil finish or water sealer such as Thompson's Wood Protector or CWF. Clear surface finishes are too brittle and tend to crack.

ACADIA BENCH AND CHAIR

Giving the Classic Garden Bench a Whorl

The genesis of this design is this: English garden benches are everywhere. College campuses. Public parks. Private yards. They're sold in mail-order catalogs. In deck and landscaping showrooms. Furniture stores. Even department stores. So we couldn't very well create the definitive outdoor furniture project book without an Americanized English-style garden bench.

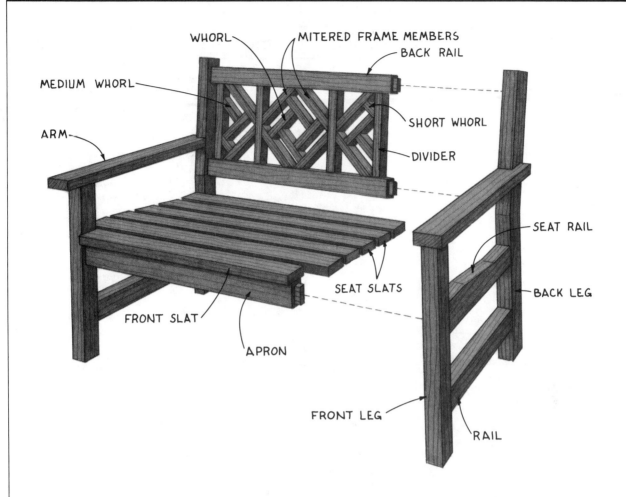

WHORL

MITERED FRAME MEMBERS

BACK RAIL

MEDIUM WHORL

SHORT WHORL

ARM

DIVIDER

SEAT RAIL

BACK LEG

FRONT SLAT

SEAT SLATS

APRON

FRONT LEG

RAIL

SHOPPING LIST—BENCH

LUMBER
2¾ bd. ft. 4/4 white oak
12¼ bd. ft. 5/4 white oak
13½ bd. ft. 8/4 white oak

HARDWARE AND SUPPLIES
1 box #6 × 1⅝″ galvanized drywall-type screws
Resorcinol glue

FINISH
Exterior-grade penetrating oil, such as CWF

SHOPPING LIST—CHAIR

LUMBER
1⅓ bd. ft. 4/4 white oak
7⅛ bd. ft. 5/4 white oak
12¼ bd. ft. 8/4 white oak

HARDWARE AND SUPPLIES
25 pcs. #6 × 1⅝″ galvanized drywall-type screws
Resorcinol glue

FINISH
Exterior-grade penetrating oil, such as CWF

CUTTING LIST—BENCH

PIECE	NUMBER	THICKNESS	WIDTH	LENGTH	MATERIAL
Whorls	14	¾"	1"	6"	4/4 oak
Medium whorls	2	¾"	1"	5"	4/4 oak
Short whorls	2	¾"	1"	3½"	4/4 oak
Mitered frame members	16	¾"	1"	8½"	4/4 oak
Dividers	6	¾"	1"	12"	4/4 oak
Back rails	2	1⅛"	2½"	54½"	5/4 oak
Back legs	2	1¾"	4½"	34"	8/4 oak
Front legs	2	1¾"	2½"	22¾"	8/4 oak
Rails	2	1¾"	2¼"	17½"	8/4 oak
Seat rails	2	1¾"	3"	17½"	8/4 oak
Arms	2	1¾"	3"	23½"	8/4 oak
Apron	1	1¾"	3"	54½"	8/4 oak
Seat slats	5	1⅛"	2⅞"	56½"	5/4 oak
Front slat	1	1⅛"	2⅞"	53"	5/4 oak

CUTTING LIST—CHAIR

PIECE	NUMBER	THICKNESS	WIDTH	LENGTH	MATERIAL
Whorls	6	¾"	1"	6"	4/4 oak
Medium whorls	2	¾"	1"	5"	4/4 oak
Short whorls	2	¾"	1"	3½"	4/4 oak
Mitered frame members	8	¾"	1"	8½"	4/4 oak
Dividers	4	¾"	1"	12"	4/4 oak
Back rails	2	1⅛"	2½"	30"	5/4 oak
Back legs	2	1¾"	4½"	34"	8/4 oak
Front legs	2	1¾"	2½"	22¾"	8/4 oak
Rails	2	1¾"	2¼"	17½"	8/4 oak
Seat rails	2	1¾"	3"	17½"	8/4 oak
Arms	2	1¾"	3"	23½"	8/4 oak
Apron	1	1¾"	3"	30"	8/4 oak
Seat slats	5	1⅛"	2⅞"	32"	5/4 oak
Front slat	1	1⅛"	2⅞"	28½"	5/4 oak

But what should it look like?

Some are very plain, with heavy legs, slatted backs, bulky arms. Others are ornate, with broadly rounded contours and scrollwork backs. Embellished with carving, perhaps. One design purports to reflect the intricacies of herbal knot gardens. Phil Gehret had built a handsome garden bench a few years back, but it was pretty plain, so we opted for something a bit more stylish this time. The stylishness we settled on was inspired by, of all things, a fence. It's the fence you see in the photo, which is the fence Phil built around his patio a few years ago.

The finished chair and bench are large, heavy, solid, and spacious. Just what garden seating should be.

The setting I've always envisioned for these pieces is not a brick patio, but the grass under a huge oak tree. The long view is to a huge pond, edged by wooded hills and, at its far end, two granite domes. The pond is Jordan Pond, the granite domes are The Bubbles. The setting is in Maine's Acadia National Park. The picture is vivid enough and persistent enough that the chair and bench are labeled "Acadia."

And the best part, if you like irony, is that Acadia is the name the French gave their sixteenth-century colony that encompassed what is now Maine, New Brunswick, and Nova Scotia. A French-American name for an English garden bench. Perfect.

Builder's Notes

The single dominating characteristic of this project is the mortise-and-tenon joint. If my quick count is correct, the chair alone has 48 of them. I mention this not to scare you away from this project, but to focus on equipment. With the right tools, you can knock these joints out almost as easily as rabbet-and-dado joints.

Materials. The stock used in building the chair and bench is white oak. White oak is a strong, heavy American native. Teak is the traditional material of garden benches, but it seems an endangered material. And we're building an American garden bench here.

A plus for oak in this project is that it is hard and stands up well in mortise-and-tenon joints. In addition, white oak is a good choice for an outdoor project, since it is rot resistant.

Alternatives include the outdoor standbys, redwood and cedar. Both of these are rot resistant, but both are soft and will be less satisfactory given the number of mortise-and-tenon joints involved in the project. These woods will yield more lightweight pieces, which can be a plus.

Other materials aren't called for. Well, some resorcinol to glue the parts together, a couple of screws to attach the parts to the back legs, a quart of finish. But that's it.

Tools and techniques. A hollow-chisel mortising attachment for the drill press is what you need to build this chair and bench. If you don't have one, get one. Break it in on this project.

Especially if you tend to be a power-tool woodworker, the mortise is an obstacle. The traditional technique for mortising involves a fair amount of handwork, paring the walls of mortises that have been roughed out with a drill. A drill press enables you to bore the holes quickly and uniformly, but you still have to cut away the ridges left between the holes; it is still handwork.

The glory of the mortising attachment is that it bores a square hole. Setup is no more time-consuming than setting up to rough the mortises, and the drill press

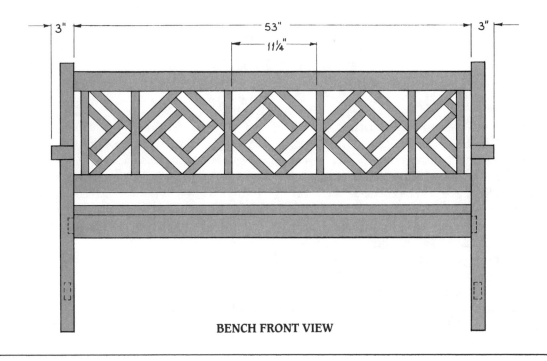

BENCH FRONT VIEW

CHAIR PLAN VIEWS

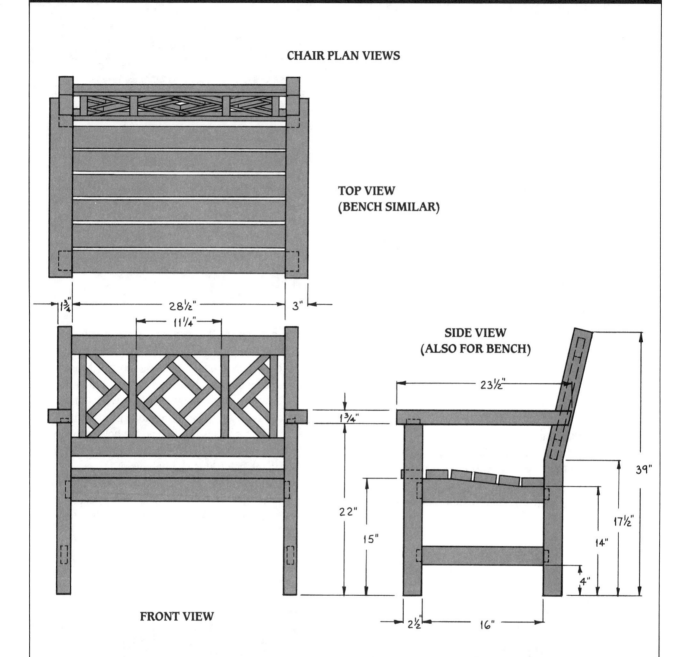

TOP VIEW
(BENCH SIMILAR)

SIDE VIEW
(ALSO FOR BENCH)

FRONT VIEW

work is all the work there is. When you retract the quill and switch off the drill press motor, the mortise is done.

The mortising attachment consists of a cast-iron yoke that holds a hollow chisel, the chisel and a special auger bit that fits inside, and a fence and hold-downs that secure the workpiece. The yoke, which is split to accommodate the chuck, attaches to the quill and holds the hollow chisel just below the chuck. The chisel fits into a socket in the yoke, and the auger is inserted into the bottom of the chisel and slid up into the chuck. The fence/hold-down is bolted to the drill press table and adjusted to hold the workpiece tightly to the table in just the right fore-and-aft alignment.

To "drill" a mortise, you pull on the quill feed, lowering the chisel to the wood. It's hard to tell, but the auger actually contacts the wood first, boring a round hole and augering the waste chips up and out of the hole. The chisel hits the wood second, just a hair behind the auger, and squares the hole. The waste it cuts is augered out with the rest of the waste. The hold-down comes into play as you retract the quill; it holds the workpiece tightly so you can pull the tightly wedged chisel out of it.

Several sizes of chisels are available. The ⅜-inch chisel, which probably gets the most use in our shop, makes a ⅜-inch-square hole. Cutting a full mortise invariably involves boring a row of holes, sometimes two or three rows of holes. As you skim through the directions for this project, I think you'll find that the ⅜-inch chisel was used exclusively.

Other than the mortiser, the essential tool is a table saw with a 1½- to 2-horsepower motor and a sharp blade. Ripping 8/4 (eight-quarter) oak can bog a lesser machine. A dado cutter to fit the table saw will expedite the cutting of tenons.

1. **Prepare the stock.** To prepare your hardwood for use, you need to joint and plane it to reduce it to working thicknesses and to smooth the faces and edges. Following the "Cutting List," crosscut the boards to rough working lengths first, and mark each piece so you know what its intended use is. (Of course, you'll have to remark them before long, since dressing the boards will remove your labels.)

To dress each board, smooth one face on the jointer, then joint one edge. Run the board through the planer as many times as is required to reduce it to the desired thickness. (When planing a lot of parts of a common thickness, the usual practice is to set the cutters, run all of them through, reset the cutters and run them all through again, and so forth. That way, all the boards will end up at the same thickness.) Finally, rip the boards to within 1/16 inch of the final width, then trim away that last 1/16 inch and at the same time smooth away the saw marks on the jointer.

The result is a board whose surfaces are flat and at right angles to their neighbors, and whose faces are parallel to each other.

There are some alternatives, although the results won't always be ideal. The best alternative, if you lack a jointer and planer, is to buy from a lumberyard or dealer that can surface the boards to your specifications.

2. **Make the back inserts.** The diamond-whorl back inserts are composed of many small pieces, all of which are mortised and tenoned. Making the inserts is not difficult so much as tedious. Given the number of mortises that must be cut—the chair back alone has 32 mortises—a hollow-chisel mortising attachment is a virtual necessity.

The only difference between the chair and the bench, as far as the back inserts go, is the number of full diamond whorls. The chair has a single full whorl and two halves, the bench has three full whorls and the two halves.

Begin by trimming the various whorls, mitered frame members, and dividers to the lengths specified by the "Cutting List." Check the *Back Insert Parts Layout* and, as you trim the pieces to length, miter the ends of the appropriate parts.

Cut the tenons on these pieces next. No particular layout on the pieces is necessary; it's all in the tool setups. Set the table saw's rip fence to govern the length of the tenons first. Adjust the depth of cut, and with the workpieces cradled one by one in the miter gauge, trim away the waste. Make three or four passes to cut one face of each tenon. To cut the angled tenons, simply adjust the angle of the miter gauge; the position of the rip fence remains unchanged. The corners of the latter tenons are trimmed away on the band saw.

The whorls have a square-cut tenon on each end. The mitered frame members have mitered tenons on

Cut the tenons on the mitered frame members on the table saw. Adjust the rip fence to govern the length of the tenon, and set the miter gauge to the miter angle. Two or three passes over the saw blade should complete each face.

Lay out the mortises on all the whorls at the same time. Line them up side by side, align them with a square, as shown, then scribe lines across all of them. Marking the ends of the mortises is sufficient, since your drill press setup will orient the mortises uniformly across the width of the piece.

BACK INSERT PARTS LAYOUT

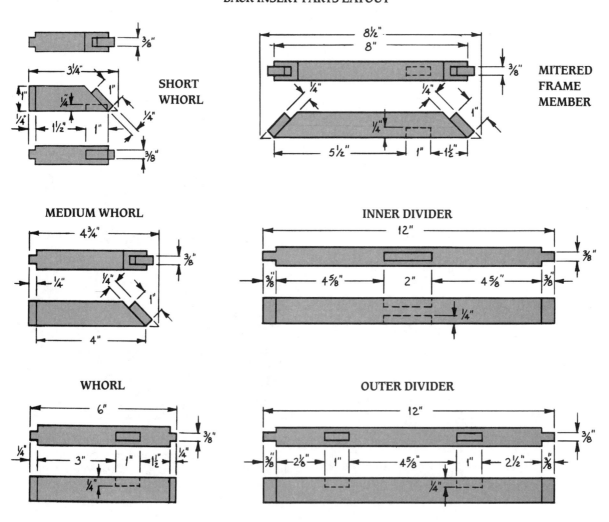

SHORT WHORL

MITERED FRAME MEMBER

MEDIUM WHORL

INNER DIVIDER

WHORL

OUTER DIVIDER

TIP

The short whorls are *so* short that you may be better off cutting the tenons on them by hand. Lay out these tenons with a pencil and square, then cut them with a backsaw.

---

both ends. The short and medium whorls have one square-cut tenon and one mitered tenon.

Cut the mortises next. The mortises are all the same width—⅜ inch—and are all centered across the width of the parts. The tool setup thus is the same for all the parts. What changes is the length of the mortises,

and this is what you need to mark on the various parts. Scribe lines across the parts to indicate the position and length of the mortises. On one piece, lay out the sides of the mortise, and use this piece to set up the mortiser.

Next, install the mortising attachment and ⅜-inch mortising chisel on your drill press. Mount the fence on the drill press table and adjust it to properly position the mortise. Drill a test or two to refine the setup. When the setup is satisfactory, drill the mortises in all the parts. (When you cut the mortises in the short whorls, you'll discover that they cut into the mitered tenons, creating a small hollow and perhaps even causing a section of the tenon to break off. The assembly will still go together, so don't worry about it.)

$3.$ **Cut the back rails and assemble the back.**
The two back rails are virtually identical, with tenons to join them to the side frames, and mortises for the various tenons of the back inserts. The inserts are flush with the front faces of the rails, so the mortises must be offset toward the front (the rails are thicker than the insert parts).

Following the *Back Rail Layout,* mark the location and lengths of the mortises on one edge of each rail. As with the back insert parts, you need only mark the ends

of each mortise, not the sides. After marking the mortises, mark the front face of each rail. The most direct approach: Set the two rails beside each other, marked edge to marked edge, and write "front" on the face of each.

Use the same setup to drill these mortises that you used to mortise the back insert parts. You will have to adjust the hold-down, of course, to accommodate the rails, which are wider than the back insert parts were. Be sure you set the rail's front against the fence when you do the mortising.

BACK RAIL LAYOUT

CHAIR

SETTEE

After cutting the mortises, tenon the ends of the rails. This operation can be performed on the table saw. Adjust the fence to govern the length of the tenons (¾ inch from the outside of the blade), set the depth of cut (to ³⁄₁₆ inch), and guide the rail with the miter gauge. The tenons are shouldered on both faces and edges. You can switch from your regular blade to a dado cutter to expedite the tenoning operation.

Assemble the back rails and the whorls. Carefully sand the sawed edges, and finish sand all the parts.

Before mixing the glue, however, do a dry run. This will give you a chance to ensure that everything fits as you want it to. Assuming all the joints do fit properly, pull the assembly apart and mix a batch of resorcinol glue. Resorcinol has a long "open time," meaning that it doesn't dry quickly. In practical terms, this means you can work deliberately, taking the time to be neat, to get all the little whorl parts assembled. You don't have to rush. Use a rubber mallet, if necessary, to drive joints closed; the rubber won't mar the wood.

The diamond-whorl inserts have to be assembled in sequence, as demonstrated in this dry run. *Top left:* The central cluster is created by joining one whorl to the second, then joining a third to a fourth. The resulting two elements can be pressed together, forming the central cluster. *Top right:* Next, you add the mitered frame members, as shown. *Bottom:* Finally, you add the dividers. Assemble additional inserts in the same sequence and add them to the first. When all are joined, add the top and bottom rails to tie the whole works together.

The joints between the inserts and the rails are more likely than the others in this project to hold moisture. Resorcinol glue will fill any gaps in fit, and will seal the joint against moisture. Resorcinol also is runny and stains, so the real trick is to apply enough glue to really seal the joint while avoiding overflow that will mar the wood.

4. Cut the parts for the side frames. Cut the legs, rails, and seat rails to the sizes specified by the "Cutting List."

Normally, it is easier to make joinery cuts in a board before you cut it to an irregular shape. The back legs of this project are an exception to the general rule; the shape must be cut before the mortises. Lay out each back leg, as shown, on a 34-inch-long board. Note the grain direction. The layout shown minimizes the width of board needed. The trick is to locate the bend in the leg first, then methodically to extend the layout from that point. Cut out each leg on the band saw.

BACK LEG LAYOUT

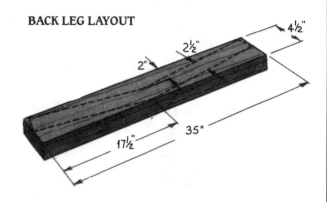

5. Cut the mortises. Whether you are building the chair or the bench, the general procedure is the same. Lay out the side assembly parts on a flat work surface. Lay out the mortises, as shown in the *Side Frame Joinery* drawing. You do need to completely lay out at least one mortise on each face of one leg to help set up the mortiser. Otherwise, you need only mark the ends of each mortise, since the setup will control the sides.

Use the mortising attachment to cut these mortises. Since all are ¾ inch wide, you can use the same ⅜-inch hollow chisel you used in previous steps. The mortises for the seat rails and stretchers can be cut in the front and back legs with a single setup, so do these first. To set up, set a front leg against the fence, then loosen the fence bolts. Lower the chisel to the workpiece and jockey the workpiece forward and back until you have the chisel properly positioned across the width of the stock. Tighten the fence bolts.

To cut the mortise, bore a series of square holes that open up the mortise from one layout line to the next. Pull the workpiece away from the fence, turn it, and butt the other side to the fence. Bore a second set of holes, doubling the width of the mortise.

To cut the mortises for the back rails, adjust the fence setting. This setting will also serve for cutting the apron mortises in the front legs.

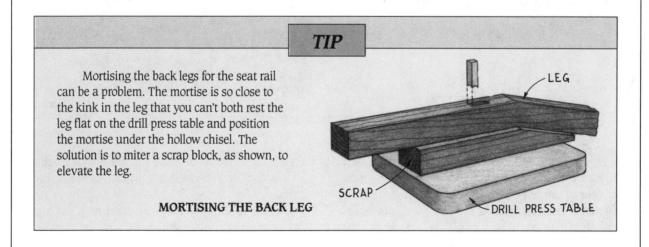

TIP

Mortising the back legs for the seat rail can be a problem. The mortise is so close to the kink in the leg that you can't both rest the leg flat on the drill press table and position the mortise under the hollow chisel. The solution is to miter a scrap block, as shown, to elevate the leg.

MORTISING THE BACK LEG

SIDE FRAME JOINERY

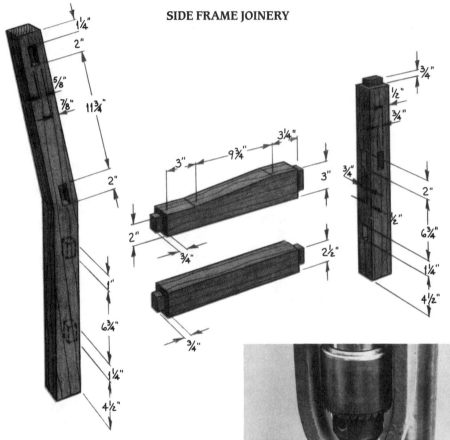

A drill press equipped with a mortising attachment can, in fact, bore a square hole. The key is the hollow chisel held by the yoke surrounding the chuck. The auger within the chisel cuts and excavates most of the waste, while the chisel simultaneously squares the sides of the hole. The hold-down attached to the fence enables you to back the chisel out of the workpiece.

6. **Tenon the rails and front legs.** The front legs are tenoned for the arm, and the rails and seat rails, of course, are tenoned for the legs. All are similarly sized. Cut them on the table saw using the same procedure used to tenon the back rails. Note here that the seat rails will have to be cut to shape after the tenons are cut, and that that operation will bring their rear tenons to the desired size.

Set the rip fence and the depth of cut, and guide the workpiece with the miter gauge. Since the mortises for these tenons are already cut, you can test your setup on a scrap and fit the tenon you cut on this scrap to one of the mortises. If the setup is dead on, cut the tenons.

Before moving to the assembly step, the seat rails need to be cut to shape on the band saw. As you can see from the *Side View,* the profile of the rails dips slightly (but gracefully) to the rear, the better to accommodate the sitter. The critical dimensions are shown, and the profile suggested. The easiest approach for you to take is to sketch your own profile using the critical dimensions as starting points. Cut the first rail, then use it as a template to lay out the second. Then carefully sand the sawed edges, and finish sand all the parts of the side assemblies.

7. Assemble the side frames.

Dry assemble and clamp each side assembly to check for fit (and to practice the clamping routine). If the fit is satisfactory, assemble both units with glue.

After the clamps are set, stand the two assemblies side by side to be sure that one of them does not lean farther back than the other. This simple precaution can save you from building a twisted seat. Adjust the clamps to make the two frames line up before the glue dries.

8. Cut and fit the arms to the side frames.

Trim the arms to the dimensions specified by the "Cutting List."

Fitting the arms to the side frame isn't too difficult if you work methodically. First, with the appropriate side frame laying on the workbench, set the arm in position, resting on the shoulder of the front leg tenon, and establish the alignment you want. Mark on the arm where it contacts the back leg. Scribe along the edge of the leg to transfer the leg's angle onto the edge of the arm. Mark along the bottom of the arm onto the back leg, too.

Using the marks as a starting point, lay out the notch on the arm. Cut it with a backsaw.

Measure from the mark on the back leg to the tenon, and transfer this measurement to the arm, marking across its bottom surface. Now set the arm in place, aligning this mark with the tenon. Trace around the tenon, then cut the second-to-last mortise in the project. Refit the arm to the side frame and refine the fit, if necessary.

Repeat the process to fit the other arm to its side frame. In the process, cut the *last* mortise of the project.

9. Cut and tenon the apron.

The last part to be cut before the chair or bench can be glued up is the apron. This is a heftier, unmortised version of the back rails. Trim it to the length specified by the "Cutting List," then cut tenons on each end. Size the tenons to fit the mortises already cut for them in the front legs.

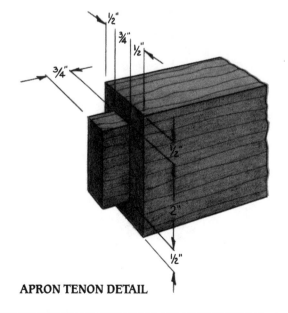

APRON TENON DETAIL

10. **Join the back assembly and the apron to the side frames.** Be sure you have a perfectly flat surface on which to set the legs as you clamp the unit together. Make a final dry run, both to make a final check of joint fits and to practice the assembly and clamping routine. If everything is satisfactory, repeat the process using glue.

Lay both side assemblies on the floor and apply glue to the mortises. Apply glue to the tenons on one end of the back assembly. Fit the tenons into their mortises. Install the apron. Spread glue on the remaining exposed tenons. With a helper, lift the assembly and insert the tenons into the mortises in the second side frame. Now set the unit on its feet and apply clamps, using cauls to prevent the steel jaws from marring the wood.

11. **Install the slats and arms.** While the glue sets, trim the seat slats to the lengths specified by the "Cutting List." Sand them. Using a ⅜-inch plug cutter, make a heap of plugs from scraps of the working stock. Try to match the color and figure of the slats.

Once the glue has dried in the frame joints, remove the clamps and install the slats. Drill countersunk and counterbored pilot holes and screw the seat slats in place. Cover the screw heads with the wooden plugs, gluing them in place. Set each plug carefully, aligning the grain in the plug with the grain of the slat. After the glue sets, pare the plugs flush and give them a touch-up pass with the finish sander.

Glue and screw the arms in place. The mortise is glued onto the tenon, of course, and a single screw is driven through the edge of the arm into the back leg. Conceal this screw beneath a wooden plug, too.

12. **Finish the bench or chair.** Sand the unit thoroughly and apply your favorite outdoor finish. Phil applied two coats of CWF, his favorite exterior-grade penetrating oil. The first coat is applied liberally and allowed to penetrate for about 20 to 30 minutes. Then, while the first coat is still wet, the second coat is brushed on. The oil needs to dry for 48 to 72 hours.